Escaping the Dark House:
A Self-Help Memoir of Depression

by William A. Peters

I0417335

"There is not one of us in whom a devil does not dwell.
At some time, at some point, that devil masters each of us.
It is not having been in the dark house, but having left it, that counts."
- Teddy Roosevelt

Table of Contents

Who This Book Is For

The following is both a memoir and self-help book. It details most of my therapy sessions and topics that came up during those sessions. I wrote it for both depression sufferers and their family and friends. However, I believe it will also be of interest and use to a general audience. Through my struggle to overcome depression I learned many lessons that I share in this book. One important lesson that I learned is that an attitude of self-help is important. It's unreasonable to expect one hour of therapy per week to implement long-term change after a lifetime of psychologically unhealthy living. A depressive has to make a conscious effort to put therapy into practice in the time between therapy sessions. The speed of improvement for a depressive is dependent on his willingness to work on himself between sessions. This book provides ideas on what to do outside therapy sessions, and what to talk about in therapy sessions. It will help you or a loved one escape the dark house called depression.

Please note that this book is not intended as a

substitute for medical advice or treatment. It is intended to be a supplement to therapy. Any person suffering from depression should consult a qualified medical practitioner or therapist.

(Note: The events of this book are my honest recollections of my past. Although my father is portrayed negatively in a few parts of the following, I love my father and we have a good relationship. This is not an attempt to hurt anyone.)

Introduction

Depression often grows in a person so slowly that neither the individual nor those close to them notice the change; it gradually becomes part of the self. The person doesn't remember and can't imagine anything other than this depressed state. I had a family background that is common among depressed men: a distant, angry father and a shallow, narcissistic mother (stepmother). My birth mother died from cancer when I was eight years old, and my father remarried not long thereafter. I felt my father and stepmother weren't interested in either me or my sister. This belief grew stronger when my stepsister arrived, and they doted on her. My other sister and I were often criticized by our parents. Because children can't see their parents objectively, they make the way their parents treat them part of themselves; if you are treated like dirt long enough, you begin to feel like dirt. Instead of understanding that father is too critical, the child experiences himself as inadequate; instead of understanding that mother is cold, the child experiences himself as unlovable. These feelings persist into adulthood as the basis for depression, an existence without hope or joy.

As early as high school I sensed there was something wrong with me, but dismissed my state as normal sadness that everyone experiences. I began to unravel when in university, which for me began in 1995. As my emotional state worsened, so did my academic performance. I had serious difficulty concentrating; I couldn't sit at my desk and study as I'd done for hours everyday during high school. I did things I never did before: gave up on courses, didn't write some exams, failed a few courses, and experimented with drugs (psychedelic mushrooms). I began to doubt that I'd graduate. Near the end of my undergraduate studies I flirted with counseling services at my university and discovered cognitive behavior therapy (CBT). I self-diagnosed myself with depression, and did some CBT exercises that I found helpful in improving my mood. I graduated in 2000 with a Bachelor of Science in physics and a minor in computer science.

After graduating from university, I went to work at a small company as an Internet software developer. I liked the work but not the company, and after six months I was fired. During that unemployment period I sought professional treatment for my depression for the first time. I saw a psychiatrist at a psychotherapy clinic once a week. He put me on a low dose of an SSRI (selective serotonin reuptake inhibitor) drug, which I found helpful. I didn't think he was a good therapist, though, so I was glad when I found another job in another city, and the therapeutic relationship ended. However, my new job was in a rural area lacking psychiatrists so I would have to rely on my SSRI drug and CBT exercises for as long as I stayed at this job. This second job lasted six months, with my employer terminating my employment. I moved back to the city of my university and resumed therapy with a second psychiatrist from South Africa. He was the best of the three that have treated me. I saw him for about four months before I accepted another job, and moved to South Korea in 2002. My SSRI medicine ran out, and because I was unfamiliar with the medical system in Korea, I went without for years. I eventually found an English-speaking doctor at the international center of a large hospital and she put me on a 20 mg dose of Prozac, which was helpful. At that time I had just started my first office job as a technical editor at a small IP law firm, but was having difficulty adapting to the environment. I had difficulty concentrating, and was worried that I might be fired for lack of productivity (I heard rumors that my manager said I wasn't working hard enough). Prozac changed all that. I ended up outlasting all of my Korean coworkers at that firm (I was the last of my department to be laid off after three years). In the years following that job I took Prozac regularly and looked for an affordable, English-speaking therapist. It wasn't until the fall of 2013 that I found Dr. Lee at Seoul National University Hospital in Seoul, South Korea. I've been seeing him for talk therapy sessions on Saturday mornings since then. I am now a 40-year-old married man with two children, a career as a technical editor, and depression. I believe that most psychiatrists would classify me as a "high-functioning depressive."

Depression Defined

Many people confuse sadness and depression, I was one of them. Sadness is a normal emotion created by realistic perceptions describing a negative event involving loss or disappointment in an undistorted way. Depression, however, is an illness that always results from thoughts that are distorted in some way.

Either depression or sadness can develop after a loss or failure in your efforts to reach a goal of great personal importance. Sadness comes without distortion. It involves a flow of feeling and therefore has a time limit. It never involves a lessening of your self-esteem. Depression is frozen--it tends to persist or recur indefinitely, and always involves loss of self-esteem. When a depression clearly appears after an obvious stress, such as ill health, the death of a loved one, a divorce, or a business reversal, it is sometimes called a "reactive depression." At times it can be difficult to identify the stressful event that triggered the episode. Those depressions are often called "endogenous" because the symptoms seem to be generated entirely out of thin air. In both cases, however, the cause of the depression is identical--distorted, negative thoughts. It has no adaptive or positive function whatsoever, and represents one of the worst forms of suffering.

Depression is classified as a mood disorder. Research makes it clear that depression can be inherited. For several decades, researchers in epidemiology, the science of tracking the course of disease, have been able to demonstrate that major depression runs genetically in families. By taking close family histories, and by studying identical twins raised in different settings, investigators have shown that there is a strong genetic component to major depression, independent of one's environment.

Given the right mix of chromosomes, any boy or girl, will have a susceptibility to this disease. But in the majority of cases, biological vulnerability alone is not enough to bring about the disorder. It is the collision of inherited vulnerability with psychological injury that produces depression. It begins with subtle indications: more crankiness and irritability before the sad, hopeless mood takes over. Once the black cloud descends, there follows a loss of interest in activities that were sources of pleasure, decreased energy, lethargy, a poor appetite with weight loss, lessened or no interest in sex, withdrawal from social interactions, an unreasonable feeling of guilt or worthlessness, an impaired ability to concentrate and make decisions, and perhaps thoughts or even plans to commit suicide.

The previously described condition is the classic form of depression most people think of. Although many men may be reluctant to admit that they are suffering from overt depression, the disorder itself has been recognized since ancient times. As early as the fourth century B.C., Hippocrates, "the father of medicine," reported a condition whose symptoms included "sleeplessness, irritability, despondency, restlessness, and aversion to food"--a description of overt depression easily recognizable today. Hippocrates saw the malady as caused by an imbalance of black bile, one of the four humors, and he therefore named the disease simply "black bile," which in Greek reads "melanae chole", or melancholia.

Overt depression preys upon men, women, and sometimes children from all walks of life, all classes, and all cultures. Epidemiologists have found descriptions resembling overt depression throughout the world-- both in developed and in developing societies. And the number of overtly depressed people seems to be on the rise. Researcher Myrna Weissman and her colleagues checked medical records going back to the beginning of the century. They calculated that, even allowing for increased reporting, each successive generation has doubled its susceptibility to depression. Such trends were corroborated worldwide in a random sampling of

39,000 subjects from such diverse countries as New Zealand, Lebanon, Italy, Germany, Canada, and France. Researchers have found depression in greater numbers and at earlier ages than ever before throughout the world. The National Institute for Mental Health reports that in the United States somewhere between 6 and 10 percent of the U.S. population is battling some form of this disease.

The types of depression:

- Endogenous depression. This type of depression is genetic and neurobiological; people are born with it.
- Depression as a consequence of attachment problems or abuse. This type of depression is a consequence of an early life loss or adversity, or failure of parents to provide a secure base and safe haven for the developing child.
- Situational or stress-induced depression. Serious, chronic stress can deplete the brain of critical neurotransmitters and thus over sensitize it to stress--the outcome being a persistent depression.
- Post-traumatic stress depression. This type of depression is the outcome of traumatic stress occurring after childhood--accident, injury, natural disaster, medical trauma, or combat-related trauma.

I believe that I suffer from type 2 depression, although endogenous depression is also a possibility (both my father and grandfather suffered from depression so my depression could be genetic). I may have both; maybe I was born with a genetic predisposition to depression that manifested itself after the childhood adversity I experienced. I also believe that my friend Paul, who I mention later in the book, also suffers from type 2 depression. In detail: "[Depressives with a history of childhood neglect or abuse] frequently display a tendency toward remarkable, dramatic shifts of mood from feeling okay to feeling seriously depressed. Such depression also manifests itself in a cognitive 'default mode' of negative expectations about the world--no one is going to surprise this person with a positive outcome. People with this type of depression also appear unable to calm down or 'self-soothe' in times of challenge. They tend to plunge into despair whenever minor upsets occur. And when they plunge, they may engage in impulsive self-injurious behavior such as drinking, gambling, risky sexual escapades, or even suicide. ... Over the course of life, the way people habitually think about themselves develops into self-image. The self-image that emerges from an implicit memory of despair is an intrinsic sense of worthlessness. The trigger to plunging into this kind of depression can be any situation, inner thought or conversation that elicits fear of being disappointed, abandoned, or neglected. In some cases, the trigger may be obvious, such as a failure to receive a hoped-for promotion, but other times it can be something as small as not receiving attentive service by waitstaff at a restaurant.[1]"

[1] 10 Best-Ever Depression Management Techniques by Margaret Wehrenberg

Freud's Free Association

Therapy session: 5 April 2014

Today I met with Dr. Lee for talk therapy. He is a tall, thin, soft-spoken, thirty-something Korean male. He seems to be both younger than me (I'm 39) and an inexperienced psychiatrist, but he is friendly and speaks English well. We meet every Saturday morning at 10 a.m. in an office in the psychiatry department of Seoul National University Hospital. The offices are soulless places with a desk, computer, chairs, fake flowers, a sink that seems to be rarely used, and a long window allowing a view of the hospital roof. Unhappy Korean patients and family members sit in the hall outside the offices waiting. There is a nurse sitting at a computer in the hall who tells them it's their turn to slide open the door for a session with one of the psychiatrists practicing there. I occasionally hear one of the female patients shouting and wailing in a nearby office.

Today I talked with Dr. Lee about free association. He thinks that I am editing myself in session, and that I should stop doing it and just say what's on my mind. We also talked about my getting upset at the end of last week's session (I cried at the end of the session). I said that I didn't know why I had such an emotional reaction, and that it seemed disproportionate to the situation. He thought the reaction was frustration; frustration with free association.

Postscript: In a following session, Dr. Lee said that my crying in session showed that I have a difficulty with criticism.

Free Association

"Unexpressed emotions will never die. They are buried alive and will come forth later in uglier ways." - Sigmund Freud

Sigmund Freud developed the technique of free association from 1892-1895 as an alternative to hypnosis. Freud is best known as the father of psychoanalysis. Born in 1856, he was a physiologist, medical doctor and psychologist who spent most of his life in Vienna, Austria. He developed revolutionary ideas about the unconscious mind, repression, dream interpretation, and talk therapy.

Free association is considered to be the most important process of psychoanalysis. It is a process in which the patient says everything that comes to their mind--without censoring, without filtering, and without judgment. Neither therapist nor patient knows in advance exactly where the conversation will lead, but it tends to lead to material that matters to the patient. This technique is intended to help the patient learn more about what she thinks and feels, in an atmosphere of non-judgmental curiosity and acceptance. The goal of free association is not to unearth specific answers or memories, but to instigate a journey of co-discovery that can enhance the patient's integration of thought, feeling, and self-hood.

Free association is considered essential to psychoanalysis because it is how the unconscious reveals itself. The idea of this therapy is to recline, drift into that more dream-like state in which we recall forgotten feelings and memories, where we gain access to deeper sensations, fantasies, anxieties, and longings, and free associate. Then, at the end of each session, the therapist gives a brilliant, all-encompassing, earth-shattering interpretation of your behavior. You walk away more self-actualized, and hopefully implement healthy changes in your life that make you happier. That's the ideal, but not always the reality.

Covert Depression

Therapy session: 24 May 2014

I read another book on depression recently, and it was enlightening. I saw a lot of the behaviors of the males of my father's family in the book: alcoholism, rageaholism, and love addiction, to name a few. I think my addictions have been: spending, electronic gaming, and sex. I think my father and I suffer from the covert depression described in the book. I believe my grandfather did as well.

As other fathers have done to their sons, my father--through the look in his eyes, the tone of his voice, the quality of his touch--- passed the depression he did not know he had on to me just as surely as his father had passed it on to him. A chain of pain, linking parent to child across generations, a toxic legacy. My father's depression was born from the pain he experienced as a little boy--hundreds of small instances of betrayal, abandonment, and abuse. For those with a biological vulnerability to disorder, such moments can become the building blocks of depression, a condition which, conceived in the boy, erupts later on in the man.

My father's unrecognized pain resided inside him like a bomb, waiting for its appointed time. The force of its ticking pushed him from his family. It sped him toward mood buffers and self-esteem enhancers like alcohol, love addiction and occasional violence. In his efforts to escape his own depression, my father let himself sink into behaviors-- irritability, dominance, drinking, and emotional unavailability-- that pushed away the very people whom he most loved and needed. He is once again single and unhappy, does not understand why, and likely will not get help.

Lately I've been over-concerned with my father's welfare. I recently learned that he plans to sell his house that he has been co-habiting with his third wife and separate from her. I predicted that this would result in him sinking into overt depression or succumbing to love addiction again. I had three conversations with my two sisters and an aunt because of my concern. I was agitated and anxious but I've managed to calm myself (something I was poor at as a young man).

Covert Depression

"Depression is the most unpleasant thing I have ever experienced ... It is that absence of being able to envisage that you will ever be cheerful again. The absence of hope. That very

deadened feeling, which is so very different from feeling sad. Sad hurts but it's a healthy feeling. It is a necessary thing to feel. Depression is very different." - J.K. Rowling

A great many men conceal their condition from the outside world, and those close to them-- loved ones, doctors, even psychotherapists--may miss a diagnosis of overt depression. Some not only manage to camouflage their condition from those around them; they manage to hide it even from themselves. A great many men never make it into the official roll call of the depressed because their overt depression remains undiagnosed. But other men fail to get help because their expression of the disease does not fit the classic model. It is what some psychiatrists call "covert depression," "masked depression," "underlying characterological depression," and a "depression equivalent." It is hidden from those around the man, and it is largely hidden from his own conscious awareness.

Yet it nevertheless drives many of his actions. Hidden depression drives several of the problems we think of as typically male: physical illness, alcohol and drug abuse, domestic violence, failures in intimacy, and self-sabotage in careers. Men tend to externalize pain; they are more likely to feel victimized by others and to discharge distress through action. A depressed man's tendency to extrude pain often does more than simply impede his capacity for intimacy. It may render him psychologically dangerous. Too often, a wounded boy grows up to become a wounding man, inflicting upon those closest to him the very distress he refuses to acknowledge within himself. Depression in men, unless it is dealt with, tends to be passed along to the next generation.

A Disturbing Thought

Therapy session: 7 June 2014

For at least the second time I've had thoughts of harming my child. I was in the kitchen at the table with my son cutting cheese when the thought came into my mind to stab my son with the knife. I was really bothered by the thought so I put the knife in the sink. I checked out some books on obsessive compulsive disorder (OCD), and found my situation described in one book, so I was relieved to not be the only one to have such a disturbing thought. (The patient in the book described having the compulsive thought to drown her daughter when bathing her. She was so worried about the thought that thereafter she invited a family member or friend over whenever she bathed her daughter, to stop her in case she followed through with the thought.)

I told my therapist in session today about the thought. He didn't seem concerned about it. He said that I should just consider it another worrisome thought that I can dismiss. I did feel relieved after dismissing the thought as "OCD" before our session. I also told him I considered not telling him about the thought as I was concerned about how he might react. I was afraid that he might think that I was a danger to my children, and take them away from me. He said that if he thought any situation that I described was dangerous, he would tell me. That reduced my anxiety.

Dealing with Intrusive Thoughts

"We suffer more often in imagination than in reality." - Seneca

Millions of people are troubled by recurrent, unpleasant thoughts, such as contemplating some horrendous act of violence against a loved one. The problem is not that you are having intrusive thoughts. Your problem is that you are evaluating them, trying to suppress them and avoid situations that evoke them. People with the "bad thoughts" form of obsessive-compulsive disorder (OCD) often avoid things that could trigger these thoughts or being in situations where they might be at risk for acting on a thought. So, for example, someone might avoid using knives, as I considered doing in response to my intrusive thought. In situations they can't avoid, they may turn to rituals, such as repetitive counting, or compulsive prayer to prevent anything bad from happening. The problem is not the intrusive thought—it's what you do about the thought. Keep these points in mind:

- Everyone has intrusive thoughts.
- Thoughts are not reality.
- Thought-suppression doesn't work. (It leads to thought rebound.)

Research on people without anxiety disorders shows that almost 90% of them have intrusive thoughts—thoughts about contamination, harm, religious impropriety, losing control, sexual "perversion", etc. So, your intrusive thoughts might mean nothing about you other than that you have a good imagination. The next time you experience and intrusive thought, remember that there is a difference between a thought and an action, and don't waste your time trying to push the thought out of your mind. Just let it come and go.

Tired of Being Tired

Therapy session: 14 June 2014

Today my psychiatrist suggested that I try a second medication to help combat my lethargy. I agreed and for at least the next two weeks I'll be taking 150 mg Wellbutrin tablets in addition to 20 mg capsules of Prozac. He also suggested that I come up with a substitute behavior instead of retreating to my bed. For years I've been retreating to my bed when I have nothing else that I'd like to do. For many years while I was single I followed the routine of going to bed when I arrived home after a day of work, often without even eating dinner. I'd usually wake up between 12-4 a.m., and not be able to get back to sleep. I'd usually read until I feel tired enough to go back to sleep. Sometimes I couldn't get back to sleep so I would get up and start my day early (sometimes at 6 a.m.). Several people, friends, aunts, my wife, and others, noticed and commented on the behavior. I usually responded by saying, "for me sleeping is not just a biological requirement, it's a hobby! I enjoy sleeping."

Joking aside, I don't think it's a healthy habit. I also noticed that my friend Paul, who I believe also suffers from depression, also often retreats to his bed. He has similar rationalizations. "It's important to get enough sleep. These days most people don't get enough sleep," he says.

"True but that doesn't justify your spending most of your days asleep. There's also such a thing as getting too much sleep," I respond.

Lethargy

Many depressives live in a haze of television, sleep or fatigue. They are stuck in the lethargy cycle detailed below. This causes them to miss out on a lot of opportunities. But, for the depressed person, opportunities are often considered challenges to be avoided.

The Lethargy Cycle is defined as self-defeating negative thoughts that make the depressive feel miserable. Painful emotions in turn convince her that her distorted, pessimistic thoughts are actually valid. Similarly, self-defeating thoughts and actions reinforce each other in a circular manner. The unpleasant consequences of procrastination make her problems even worse.

"The lethargy that occurs in depression is misleading. When we are not depressed, tiredness means that we need to rest. This rest refreshes us. The fatigue of depression, however, is often not normal tiredness; it may call not for rest but for increased activity, if only for a short while. Rest can worsen the fatigue. Part of taking care of ourselves in such moments is to stay in the flow of life, to keep participating in normal activities, even if our mood and thoughts seem to say there's no point."[2]

That is, the depressive needs to transform the lethargy cycle into a productivity cycle.

Comorbid Insomnia

"A ruffled mind makes a restless pillow." - *Charlotte Bronte*

"Comorbid" just means present simultaneously in a patient. For many years, I had depression comorbid with insomnia. I don't think I currently suffer from insomnia, but recurrence is always a possibility, so I monitor my sleep habits. Generally, insomnia is disturbed sleep that's persistent (lasts more than a month) and that causes other problems. These problems include fatigue, mental "cloudiness", mood problems, or the worsening of the symptoms of another condition, such as pain, anxiety, or depression.

"When an insomnia disorder is present for six

---

[2] The Mindful Way Through Depression: Freeing Yourself From Chronic Unhappiness by Mark Williams, John Teasdale, Zindel Segal, and John Kabat-Zinn

months or more, it's called chronic insomnia. Chronic insomnia is a problem for approximately ten percent of American adults.Comorbid insomnia is twice as common as sleep problems that occur in the absence of another condition."[3]

In the past it was assumed that comorbid insomnia was simply a symptom of the other medical or psychiatric disorder. It was assumed that the insomnia would get better when the medical or psychiatric condition was adequately treated. It is now known that this does not always happen. Insomnia often doesn't get better when the accompanying condition is treated. More often, the insomnia requires separate, focused treatment. It's true that depression does, in some cases, cause sleep difficulties, but over time the sleep difficulties can develop into an insomnia disorder.

"Research shows that simultaneously treating insomnia and depression results in greater improvement in both depression and insomnia symptoms, compared to treating only depression."

Prescription Drugs Used to Treat Depression

---

[3] Quiet Your Mind & Get to Sleep by Colleen E. Carney and Rachel Manber

Keep in mind that the use of antidepressants is still a blend of art and science. Each practitioner has a slightly different philosophy. Doctor and patient will probably have to experiment with a few drugs and dosages before they find the right one.

Prescription drugs that I am currently on to treat my depression (generic name in parentheses):

Wellbutrin (bupropion hydrochloride): Wellbutrin is an atypical antidepressant. It selectively raises levels of dopamine in the brain. Wellbutrin is particularly helpful in boosting energy and helping people have more interest in life, as dopamine affects attention and reward feelings. It is helpful for people who are lethargic or disinterested. It takes 8 to 12 weeks to see the full effects on mood. Wellbutrin's side effects include agitation (32% of people in clinical trials taking 300-600 mg daily doses experienced this side effect), dry mouth (28%), and headache/migraine (26%). It is good for treating depression with fewer sexual side effects than other antidepressants, but you must avoid alcohol use.

Prozac (fluoxetine): Prozac is a selective serotonin reuptake inhibitor (SSRI) antidepressant. It increases serotonin activity in the brain, which regulates mood. It improves mood and helps you relax. It takes 8 to 12 weeks to see full effects on mood. Its side effects include insomnia (33% of people in clinical trials experienced this side effect), nausea (29%), and headache (21%). Abrupt cessation of Prozac will produce withdrawal symptoms. It is good for treating depression and anxiety. It is more energizing than other antidepressants, but may not be the best choice for people who have trouble sleeping.

Other drugs doctors have put me on:

Celexa (citalopram): Celexa is a selective serotonin reuptake inhibitor (SSRI) antidepressant. It increases serotonin activity in the brain, which regulates mood. It improves mood and helps you relax. It takes 8 to 12 weeks to see full effects on mood. Its side effects include nausea (21%), dry mouth (20%), and sleepiness (18%). Abrupt cessation of Celexa will produce withdrawal symptoms. It is good for treating depression and anxiety. It is less likely to cause side effects than some antidepressants, but not the best choice for people with heart or liver problems.If you are overly stimulated from an antidepressant and are having trouble sleeping, your doctor may add a small dose of a second, more sedative antidepressant at night. To treat my insomnia I've been put on:

Remeron (mirtazapine): Remeron is an atypical antidepressant. It stimulates your body to make certain chemicals in the brain, such as serotonin and norepinephrine, which regulate mood. It improves mood. Its side effects include sleepiness (54%), dry mouth (25%), and increased appetite (17%). It is adequate for treating depression and good for sleep. It is more likely to cause weight gain than other antidepressants.

Stilknox (zolpidem): Stilknox is in a class of drugs called sedative-hypnotics. It interacts with your brain to make you relaxed and sleepy. Its side effects include drowsiness (8%), dizziness (5%), sinus infection (4%). It can cause sleep-walking, sleep-driving, and sleep-eating. It is very addictive. Dependence can form after daily use for 2 weeks. It is meant for short-term treatment. It is good for falling asleep and staying asleep, but it can be habit-forming and is more likely than other sleep medicines to cause disturbing side effects.

Oleptro, Desyrel (trazodone): Trazodone is a serotonin reuptake inhibitor (SRI) antidepressant. It increases serotonin activity in the brain, which regulates mood. Trazodone differs from most sleeping pills in that it is not addictive. Commonly used in lower doses to help treat sleep problems; doses of 50 to 100 mg of Trazodone are often used. It has fewer sexual side effects than many other antidepressants. It comes as a generic medication and is cheaper than many other sleep aides. It is not as effective as other medications for depression.

Alternatives to Narcotics

I stopped taking sleeping medications years ago because I was concerned about becoming dependent on them in order to sleep. Also, I learned other non-narcotic methods to manage my sleep, and don't need the medications to maintain sleep. If you have difficulty getting to sleep or maintaining sleep, I recommend:

Leaving the bedroom

"If you're aware that your mind is overactive, leave the bedroom. Don't wait fifteen to twenty minutes if it's painfully obvious that your overactive mind will prevent you from falling asleep; in this case, leave the room immediately. The rationale is also simple: pairing active thinking with the bed will produce conditioned arousal so that the bed begins to automatically bring about this response (often without our awareness). In addition to preventing such conditioning from occurring, leaving the bedroom has the added benefit that most people's thoughts and worries dissipate when they leave the bedroom. One possible explanation is that the act of getting out of bed and walking down the hall will result in becoming more lucid and awake. While many people say that they were never asleep to begin with, often they have tiny periods of light sleep that they don't notice. Thus , you many not be as lucid as you think, and may be more prone to semiconscious types of thinking and emotional states. When you're lucid and fully awake, you'll be more apt to challenge unreasonable thoughts and worries, and better able to quell unwanted mental activity than when lying in bed half awake. ... Return to your bed only when you feel sleepy again. You may need to leave the bedroom several times before your mind gets the idea that the bed is no place to worry or rehash the events of the day." (Quiet Your Mind & Get to Sleep by Colleen E. Carney and Rachel Manber)

Tell yourself something like "I can't shut off these thoughts, so I might as well go into the living room until they stop. No sense being miserable in bed."

Choose a non-energizing activity to pass the time until you feel sleepy again. I read in a comfortable chair until I feel sleepy, and then return to my bed to try to get back to sleep.

Drugs Versus Therapy

There is evidence that depressed patients who

have a history of childhood trauma, such as the early loss of a parent or sexual or physical abuse, do not respond as well to an antidepressant as they do to psychotherapy. This finding applies to me as my mother died when I was 8-years-old and I was a victim of occasional abuse growing up.

In a large, multicenter study, Dr. Charles Nemeroff, then a professor of psychiatry at Emory and now at the University of Miami, found that for depressed adults without a history of abuse, there was a clear ranking order of treatment efficacy. Combined psychotherapy (using a form of cognitive behavior therapy) and an antidepressant (in this case, Serzone) was superior to either treatment alone.

But for those who had a history of childhood trauma, the results were strikingly different: 48 percent of these patients achieved remission with psychotherapy alone, but only 33 percent of these patients responded to an antidepressant alone. The combination of psychotherapy and a drug was not significantly better than psychotherapy alone. One explanation for the varying response is that a history of trauma early in life is strongly correlated with shrinkage of the hippocampus, a brain region critical to memory and learning. One interpretation of this study is that if a person is depressed with a compromised hippocampus, she needs the active learning that comes with psychotherapy to beat her depression.

Antidepressants alone will not suffice.

A Wasted Session

Therapy session: 28 June 2014

Today's session didn't go well. I think it was a wasted session. After another wasted session, doubts about this therapist once again enter my mind. I also noticed him checking out what looked to be Facebook during the session, which annoyed me. I'm considering looking for another therapist, but am reluctant to because I've done about 45 sessions with this therapist, and I don't want to start over with another therapist. I started the session by showing Dr. Lee one of my CBT (cognitive behavior therapy) exercises I call Thought Rephrasing (see below). It was four of my negative thoughts and my rewriting of them on a small piece of paper. I showed it to him because in a previous session he expressed concern about me doing these CBT exercises correctly. He seemed uninterested. I don't recall him making a comment on that particular exercise.

At the end of a previous session I mentioned that the mother of my steady girlfriend during my university years said to her that books may be my refuge (in response to my girlfriend's comment to her that I read alot). Dr. Lee responded by saying that that might be something to talk about in the next session. So, I talked about my reading habit this session; that is, I struggled to talk about my reading habit. I should have talked about my planned topic--procrastination. I've been procrastinating about dealing with a financial issue for years. It's an important issue that I think I need to talk about further. From now on I'm going to talk about what I think is important for me to talk about regardless of whether the topic is planned or spontaneous.

Rephrasing Thoughts

"Men are disturbed not by things, but by their opinions about them." - Epictetus

Here is my execution of the CBT exercise I call Thought Rephrasing:

Negative Thought	Distortion	Substitute Thought
I don't want to go to lunch with the new work colleague.~~70~~ 0	ER, DTP, MF	It was a good time. I'm glad that I went. 90
She's probably just bringing work	DTP, JTC	She could be bringing work to

to me. ~~70~~ 30 (At work)		others. Anyway, she's just doing her job.90
Why does she keep making the same mistakes?! 70 20 (At work)	Magn., MF	English is a second language for her. Mistakes keep me in a job. 80
This is so frustrating! They can't speak English. ~~70~~ 20	ER, DTP, MF	Speaking a second language is difficult. They are doing their best. 100
How do you feel? (No better, a bit better, or much better.) A bit better.		

Cognitive Distortions:

- Emotional Reasoning (ER): Taking your emotions as evidence for the truth.

- Discounting The Positive (DTP): Transforming neutral or even positive experiences into negative ones.

- Jumping To Conclusions (JTC): You arbitrarily jump to a negative conclusion that is not justified by the facts of the situation.

- Mental Filter (MF): Picking out a negative

detail in any situation and dwelling on it exclusively, thus perceiving that the whole situation is negative.

- Magnification (Magn.) and Minimization: Blowing things up out of proportion or shrinking them.

Other Cognitive Distortions:

- All-or-Nothing Thinking: This refers to your tendency to evaluate your personal qualities in extreme, black-or-white categories.

- Labeling and Mislabeling: Attaching a negative label to yourself or others.

- Over-generalization: You arbitrarily conclude that something that happened to you once will occur over and over again.

- Should Statements: Trying to motivate yourself by saying, "I should do this " or "I must do that."

- Personalization: Seeing yourself as the cause of some negative external event that you were not primarily responsible for.

Facing My Fear

Therapy session: 5 July 2014

Today's session was my 52nd session with Dr. Lee--the longest I've gone with a therapist. I started the session by saying that I've been thinking about ending that streak by changing therapists. I said I was frustrated after last week's session, which I felt was a wasted session. I'm still considering changing my therapist. I'm going to look for options this week.

Before today's session I decided to talk about the fear I have about returning to Canada. I said that I'm worried about not being able to get a job, and not being able to support my family. I'm procrastinating about facing my financial issue. I said that I think I'd feel better if I took action about my financial issue. He ended the session by saying something similar to: "We can talk about the changing-therapists issue in the next session, if you want to."

Procrastination

"Nothing is so fatiguing as the eternal hanging on of an uncompleted task." - William James

One of the most destructive aspects of depression is the way it paralyzes willpower. In its mildest form a depressive may simply procrastinate about doing a few odious chores. (As I write this I am struggling to fill out the application forms for my wife's spousal visa; an odious chore but not a difficult one. I started filling out the documents a week ago, and could have been done the same day.)

As the lack of motivation intensifies, virtually any activity appears so difficult that the depressive becomes overwhelmed by the urge to do nothing. Because they accomplish very little, they feel worse and worse. Not only does the depressive cut himself off from normal sources of stimulation and pleasure, but his lack of productivity aggravates his self-hatred, resulting in further isolation and incapacitation. If he doesn't recognize the emotional prison in which he is trapped, this situation can go on for weeks, months, or even years (as it did for me).

The following common mind-sets cause me to procrastinate.

- Overwhelming Yourself: You magnify a task to the degree that it seems impossible to tackle. You may assume you must do everything at once instead of breaking each job down into small, discrete, manageable units that you can complete one step at a time. You might also inadvertently distract yourself from the task at hand by obsessing about endless other things you haven't gotten around to doing yet.

- Fear of Disapproval or Criticism: You imagine that any mistake will be met with strong disapproval and criticism because the people you care about won't accept you if you are human and imperfect. The risk of rejection seems so dangerous that to protect yourself you adopt as low a profile as possible. If you don't make any effort, you can't make a mistake. (I think this happens subconsciously because I can't recall conscious thoughts of fear of disapproval or criticism.)

- Low Frustration Tolerance: You assume that you should be able to solve your problems and reach your goals rapidly and easily, so you go into a frenzied state of panic and rage when life presents you with obstacles. Rather than persist patiently over a period of time, you may retaliate against the "unfairness" of it all when things get tough, and give up completely. This is also called "entitlement syndrome" because you feel and act as if you were entitled to success, love, approval, perfect health, happiness, etc. Your frustration results from your habit of comparing reality with an ideal in your head. When the two don't match, you condemn reality. It doesn't occur to you that it might be infinitely easier simply to change your expectations than to bend and twist reality.

On Suicide

Therapy session: 13 July 2014

I found and sent an e-mail to another Korean psychiatrist this week; his nurse said that he treats patients with drugs, not talk therapy. The so-called "psycho-pharmacology" is typical in Korea. You can't treat depression (and probably any other mental illness) with only a pill. Psychiatry seems to be in its infancy in Korea. My Korean wife tells me that Koreans don't go to psychiatrists. That's probably a contributing factor to the high suicide rate here.

I decided to talk about sex in this therapy session, even though I find the topic uncomfortable. "For men everything is about sex, except sex, which is about shame, emotional absence, masculine insecurity, self-involvement, aggression, and self-destructiveness. ... The sexual arena is where men naturally play out emotional conflicts which, ultimately, are not about sex after all." [4]said psychiatrist Dr. Alon

---

[4]   If Men Could Talk, Here's What They'd Say by Alon Gratch

Gratch who specializes in treating males. Once again I left therapy with the resolve to have another conversation with my wife--this time about sex.

Suicide

"Perhaps the saddest irony of depression is that suicide happens when the patient gets a little better and can again function sufficiently." - Dick Cavett

Before the 1997 Asian financial crisis, South Korea's annual rate of suicide was much lower than the average of the other industrialized nations. But it soared in the wake of the financial crisis, and it has been getting worse ever since. South Korea has had the highest suicide rate in the industrialized world for eight consecutive years; 14,160 people committed suicide in 2012, an average of 39 people per day and a 219 percent increase from the 6,444 suicides in 2000. It's the number one cause of death for people between the ages of 10 and 30. For people in their 40s, suicide is the second most common cause of death after cancer. Among the older generations, the numbers are even more bleak. According to research by the department of Family Medicine at Hallym University, some 60 percent of Koreans who attempt suicide are suffering from depression. Yet too many people in South Korea have outdated views of psychological illness. Many think that when someone is suicidal he simply lacks a strong will to live; he's weak. There's little sympathy or interest in probing below the surface. And it's not easy to get therapy for depression in South Korea, where there is still strong societal resistance to psychological treatment.

In the United States, the number of suicides has surpassed the number of deaths from car accidents, according to the "Morbidity and Mortality Weekly Report of the Centers for Disease Control". In 2010 there were almost 34,000 deaths from car accidents, and 38,000 suicides. Even more alarming, the suicide rate for Americans in mid-life, ages 35-64, increased between 1999 and 2010 by nearly 30%. The risk of suicide in the lifetime of a person with major depression is about 6%. This is significantly higher than the approximately 1% risk of suicide in the lifetime of a person drawn from the general population.

Although friends and relatives sometimes think of depression merely as a "passing phase," there's no doubt that it's often a life-threatening condition. Many people are surprised to learn that people who aren't deeply depressed sometimes kill themselves. The belief that only clinically depressed people commit suicide is potentially dangerous because friends, relatives, and significant others may wrongly assume that a person without serious depressive symptoms is "safe" and therefore doesn't require immediate psychological attention. Yet research shows that between 13% and 41% (depending on the study) of people who commit suicide don't meet diagnostic criteria for major depression.

Dr. Aaron T. Beck reported in a study that suicidal wishes were present in approximately one-third of individuals with a mild case of depression, and in nearly three-quarters of people who were severely depressed. It has been estimated that as many as 5% of depressed patients die as a result of suicide. This is approximately twenty-five times the suicide rate within the general population. No age group, social, or professional class is exempt from suicide. Depression afflicts more women than men. More women than men attempt suicide, but more men actually kill themselves--men are four times more likely than women to take their own lives.

"Some depressives are repeatedly tormented by suicidal impulses, which they experience as frightening and painful, while others have them appear as if out of the blue, detached from emotions. The impulse to spin the wheel and drive suddenly into oncoming traffic is horribly common, though no one ever talks about it."[5]

---

[5] Undoing Depression: What Therapy Doesn't Teach You and Medication Can't Give by Richard O'Connor

Suicidal wishes are active or passive. A passive death wish exists if you would prefer to be dead, but you are unwilling to take active steps to bring this about. I sometimes have suicidal wishes, and they fall into this category.

An active suicidal wish is more dangerous. If a depressive is seriously planning an actual suicide attempt, then it's important to know the following: Is there a method? Are there plans? What specific preparations have been made? As a general rule, the more concrete and well-formulated the plans are, the more likely the person may actually make a suicide attempt. The time to seek professional help is now.

Has a suicide attempt been made in the past? If so, you should view any suicidal impulse as a danger signal to seek help immediately. For many people these previous attempts seem to be "warm-ups," in which they flirt with suicide but have not mastered the particular method they have selected. The fact that an individual has made this attempt unsuccessfully on several occasions in the past indicates an increased risk of success in the future. It is a dangerous myth that unsuccessful suicide attempts are simply gestures or attention-getting devices and are therefore not to be taken seriously.

Current thinking suggests that all suicidal thoughts or actions should be taken seriously. It can be highly misleading to view suicidal thoughts and actions as a "plea for help." Many suicidal patients want help least of all because they are 100 percent convinced they are hopeless and beyond help. Because of this illogical belief, what they really want is death. The degree of hopelessness is of the greatest importance in assessing whether an individual is at risk for making an active suicide attempt at any time. This one factor seems more closely linked with actual suicide attempts than any other.

Becoming Mindful

Therapy session: 19 July 2014

I began reading a book this week on mindfulness-based therapy (MBT), so I decided to talk about it in today's session. Instead of talking back to negative thoughts, which cognitive-based therapy teaches, in MBT you are instructed to just become aware of your thoughts.

During the week I became aware of one recurring thought--that of an aunt who I feel is often critical of me. So I talked about my thoughts about her in today's session. I don't like to be criticized; no one does, but I am especially sensitive to criticism. So is my father; like father, like son. Criticism is an anger trigger for us. My grandfather, who I believe suffered from depression for most of his life and took it to the grave with him, was the angriest person I've ever known. He was also a regular drinker (member of a private drinking club).

Depression and Anger

"Most people would rather be angry than terribly sad." - John Ratey

The more depressed a person, the more negative his view of the world. In severe depression, people can become paranoid--harboring a belief that everyone, even those closest to them, is out to cause them harm. Depressives are more likely to read malicious intent into others' actions. Because of lack of sleep, decreased energy, and a self-critical attitude--all symptoms of depression--they are more easily frustrated. Anger is unwittingly used by some depressives to wake up a "sluggish brain." Angry outbursts can be a way of self-medicating a mood disorder.

Anger is an emotion, and emotions are meant to be short-lived. But, for some people, anger persists, and through its persistence, it is harmful. This is true much more for men than for women for the following two reasons. It is more acceptable for men to display anger openly than to appear sad or depressed. Anger in men is often regarded as a sign of strength whereas appearing sad or depressed is perceived as a sign of weakness. The opposite is true for women--being depressed seems natural for women whereas public displays of anger are seen as unusual and unladylike.

Anger Addiction ("Rageaholism")

"If you do not wish to be prone to anger, do not feed the habit; give it nothing which may tend to its increase." - Epictetus

Anger addiction or "rageaholism" is the compulsive pursuit of a mood change by repeatedly engaging in episodes of rage despite adverse consequences. The behavior of rageaholics ranges from tantrums to physical abuse. They will rage compulsively without regard to the negative consequences. Compulsion or loss of control is the inability to stop expressing anger once a person has begun. The inability to control angry outbursts is a sign of rageaholism. Loss of control is a sign of addiction.

Rageaholics are frequently preoccupied with resentment and fantasies of revenge. Those thoughts sometimes rise powerfully and allow no other thoughts to enter the mind. The force of anger is sometimes irresistible and followed by action. The preoccupation with the "wrongs" of others and revenge leads to rage. These thoughts crowd out all others until life becomes chronically revenge-oriented. At that point, anger controls the person's thoughts.

Denial keeps anger addicts trapped. It is the mental process by which the addict concludes that the addiction is not the problem; it's "them." Ignorance of addiction and the inability to examine themselves work together to keep rageaholics stuck. Knowing no other way to live, anger addicts deny that there is anything wrong with them. This system of denial ensures that the process of rage and righteous indignation will continue. Righteous indignation keeps the addict's focus off himself. This is why ragers seldom are able to say, "I was wrong." The individual doesn't take responsibility for his behavior and expects to be quickly forgiven.

Depression and Alcoholism

Of people treated for major depression, nearly 40 percent will struggle with alcoholism at some point in their lives. Not only do these problems tend to happen together, there's strong evidence they create each other. Depression causes addiction, which in turn causes depression.

Depressed people often self-medicate with substances in order to feel better, only to find themselves eventually addicted. In that case, treating the substance abuse by itself is ineffective because eventually depression will cause a relapse into addiction. Unfortunately, too many therapists recognize a patient's alcoholism but miss its underlying cause (depression), or, if they recognize the cause, mistreat the problems.

When people show up at mental health centers with a substance abuse problem, a referral is often made for them to get substance abuse counseling first--get cleaned up, and then get your depression treated. The problem with that sequential treatment is that when someone suffers from both depression and alcoholism, they become so intertwined that the depression itself can undermine a person's attempt at sobriety. If a person needs to go to group therapy three times a week, but can't even get out of bed to take a shower, that's going to undermine her attempts at an outpatient chemical dependency program. Simultaneous treatment of the comorbid disorders produces the best results.

Dream Interpretation

Therapy session: 27 July 2014

We did some dream interpretation in my therapy session today. I recalled a dream during the week in which I was babysitting some children in a house and the house became a mess. I could see through the walls of the house and noticed my adult relatives (my father, aunt, and uncle, I think) returning to the house. I jumped into a bed and pretended to be asleep to avoid criticism from them about the messy house. I told Dr. Lee that I think the dream shows that I feel criticized by my family. He said that my sensitivity to criticism may be due to a fear of rejection.

Dream Research

"The interpretation of dreams is the royal road to knowledge of the unconscious activities of the mind." - Sigmund Freud

Where do we go when we go to sleep?

We do not sink into a void, but instead into a mental workshop where emotionally important information is kept active until it is saved in neural networks. Out of all new experiences of a day, what our brains retain and replay in our sleep are those bits which seem familiar, based on previous experience--particularly those that have an emotional charge. These find their way to a place in the memory network where similar experiences are stored.

While sleeping at home, we usually remember at most only the last dream of the night, and even then only if it is vivid in imagery or particularly rich in emotion. Dreams are longer, more complex in structure and more emotion-filled at the end of the night than they are in the beginning, and since we are more likely to remember the dream that we are experiencing just as we wake up, we are likely to remember the wildest one of the night.

This was established in studies in the 1960s by Carl Meier, and since then it has been confirmed many times. Fred Snyder, a psychiatrist who was the chief of the Clinical Psychobiology Laboratory at the National Institute of Mental Health, undertook a detailed study of the dreams of young adults. Snyder analyzed a data bank of 635 dreams he had collected over 250 nights. These were recorded from a sample of mostly middle-class American college students with diverse backgrounds. Most striking was the pervasiveness of the self in these college students' dreams.

"The all-important 'I' appeared in 95% of the dreams," but only rarely was the "I" alone. Family members were present in 19% of dreams, friends and acquaintances in 35%, and in 46%, the others were unknowns. There were very few popular or cult figures. Only rarely did a president or movie star appear. Even the dreamed animals were not exotic creatures, but mostly domestic pets. Most of the dreamed-about people were talking. Seventy-six percent of the dreams included some auditory imagery, most often speech, but music might also be playing, or dogs barking, or rain falling.

Snyder made another interesting observation: in addition to what is happening in the foreground, there is also more or less "continuous background accompaniment of reflections and attitudes, as well as clear evidence at times of inferential thinking, remembering, deciding, feelings of volition and, of course, emotion." Emotion is often implicit in the narrative rather than explicitly named. Snyder found feelings were only mentioned in a third of the dreams. When they were explicit, they were more often unpleasant than pleasant, with a 2:1 ratio. Fear, anxiety, and anger were the most common negative emotions present in dreams, whereas on the pleasant side, "friendliness" was number one.

During the inaction of sleep we turn inward to review and evaluate the implications of our day, and the input of those new perceptions, learnings, and--most important--emotions about what we have experienced. What we experience as a dream is the result of our brain's effort to match recent, emotion-evoking events to other similar experiences already stored in long-term memory.

One purpose of this sleep-related matching process, this putting of similar memory experiences together, is to defuse the impact of those feelings that might otherwise linger and disrupt our moods and behaviors the next day. The various ways in which the mind works--the top-level rational thinking and executive deciding functions, the middle management of routine habits of thought, and the emotional relating and updating of the organized schemas of our self-concept--are not isolated from each other. They interact. The emotional aspect, which is often not consciously recognized, drives the unconscious mental activity of sleep.

Acknowledging an Achievement

Therapy session: 23 August 2014

In today's session we talked about my book. Dr. Lee commented that I hadn't brought up in any session about my recent publishing achievement. I responded that I never thought of bringing up positive experiences in a session. I thought I was supposed to bring problems to therapy. I also said that I didn't want to be a needy patient, crossing the patient-doctor boundary and trying to get my psychiatrist to be interested in my life. He said that he didn't think I was doing that, so I responded that I would bring him a paperback copy of my book next session.

The Therapeutic Process

"Mental illness is so much more complicated than any pill that any mortal could invent" - Elizabeth Wurtzel

Psychotherapy and psychoanalysis are themselves split into many schools and factions, typically named after a founder--Freudian,

Jungian, Kleinian, Kohutian--with their own theories, terminology, journals, training programs, rules, and techniques. They each claim to be the best, but the therapeutic practice should be flexible, open-minded, and non-dogmatic.

Therapy for depression generally requires moving clients out of lethargy and into action, taking charge of cognitive habits, instilling hope, changing lifestyle, and reducing negative mood. Medication is considered a first-line approach to treatment, yet therapy is more helpful in the long run. Studies that look at the combination of medication and cognitive behavioral therapy (CBT) methods suggest that people get a faster start, feeling better after 12 weeks or so on medication plus CBT, but in the long run, many people do well utilizing CBT methods without any medication. Of those treated for depression, one third achieve remission from all symptoms. Many men avoid treatment because admitting to the pain of depression is tantamount to admitting weakness. They do not acknowledge the suffering they feel until it is far too serious and has wreaked unnecessary havoc in their lives.

How to Approach Therapists and Therapy

Schedule evaluation sessions with at least three therapists before committing to therapy with one. During the evaluation sessions with each therapist, ask them about their approach. Most therapists should have no problem talking to you at least briefly about how they see human nature, pathology, and treatment.

For instance, a psychodynamic therapist is more likely to encourage you to focus on your childhood, relational dynamics, and say "how does that make you feel?" quite a bit. A solutions-focused therapist, is less likely to focus on childhood, and more likely to ask you to discuss the present and what behaviors you can do to elicit change. A cognitive behavioral therapist is going to focus more on your thought patterns and help you see how changing those thoughts can have a direct impact on your feelings.

More importantly, though, is a personality match between therapist and client. The nature of your relationship with your therapist is far more significant in determining how much benefit you will get from treatment than any particular school of therapy they may belong to.

"Based on a careful literature review conducted in 1992, M.J. Lambert estimated that while the particular techniques employed account for only approximately 15 percent of the effectiveness of therapy, the quality of the therapeutic alliance forged between therapist and client contributes a whopping 30 percent. This is only one in a whole range of studies that would suggest it doesn't matter so much what particular brand of therapy is being used as how you feel about the person doing it. In 2001, Bruce Wampold, a former statistician who examined the outcomes of treatment of depression, supported Lambert's conclusions and reported that no one modality of treatment emerged as significantly better than any other--including CBT. More recently the American Psychological Association sponsored a task force to sort out once and for all what works in the therapy relationship. Once again, the same conclusion emerged: the consensus of several thousand studies was that the nature of the therapeutic relationship had just as much impact on whether clients improved (or failed to improve) as any particular treatment method." [6]

So, it's important to consider the question, "Is there chemistry between me and my therapist?" Of the three therapists I've been treated by, only one earned my confidence.

Have a goal going into therapy. The obvious goal is to overcome depression, but you may have other problems in your life that you want to solve (e.g., a loving relationship with your spouse, good relationships with your children, to be at peace, or genuine happiness). Many people go to therapy with the foggy notion that they want to feel better – but they aren't exactly sure what that

---

[6] Psychobabble: Exploding the Myths of the Self-Help Generation by Stephen Briers

looks like.

One of the biggest differences in whether therapy is successful is whether a person outlines his goals before he goes to therapy, or very early on in it. Don't just be in therapy, be an active participant.

You can do the following to become active in your therapy:

- Buy a notebook to carry with you throughout the week and write your thoughts, feelings, dreams and behaviors. You don't have to write a lot, but just enough that it gives you an idea of what is relevant in your life before going into your session. I prefer hand writing on paper, but you can also use a smart phone for this if you prefer.

- Plan ahead. If you're a planner like me, go a bit early to your session, and while waiting review your journal/phone and make an outline of the key points you'd like to address during the session.

- Become comfortable with silence. Good therapy should have periods of silence. Sometimes you may say something powerful and meaningful. A good therapist will use the power of silence to allow that to sink in and to hopefully elicit further exploration. Allow yourself to be silent sometimes so that you can hear what is beneath the surface.

- Feel free to disagree with your therapist. Therapists make mistakes. If your therapist wrongly interprets or misstates what you have said, correct him.

- Change the structure of your therapy, if you feel that you are not making the most of your sessions. Speak to your therapist about your concerns, and offer some suggestions as to what you would like to see change. Either they will make changes to the therapy process, or it may be time to find a new therapist.

- Finally, keep in mind that it has been a rule in Freudian treatment that analysts reveal nothing about themselves, and even within modern approaches, it is relatively rare for the therapist to speak about her own life in any detail. There is a great stress on the therapeutic relationship, and some contemporary analysts describe their emotional or "counter-transference" reactions to patients, but they still do not reveal much about their own lives.

Dream Interpretation Redux

Therapy session: 30 Aug. 2014

In today's session we did some more dream interpretation. I had a dream during the week involving my older sister and her husband. I think the dream is symbolic of my frustration with the poor relationship between my older sister and me. Dr. Lee said he thinks the dream shows my disappointment with the lack of response from my sister to my recent achievement. (I published a book, and I think my older sister didn't buy it. This is especially annoying for me as the book is about running and she is a runner.)

Also, a reference to comedy came up in the dream. I think it might be due to actor/comedian Robin Williams' recent suicide. Like me, he was suffering from depression. I discussed my feelings about his death. I said that I had mixed feelings. I said that I am glad that this happened to a celebrity because it will raise awareness of the problem of depression. I also admitted that it's not nice to be happy about someone's death. I said that I was angry with the general public;

angry because they seem to be hypocrites about depression. When a celebrity such as Robin Williams commits suicide he had a disease but when a non-celebrity commits suicide they had a character flaw; it was their fault.

Postscript: I gave Dr. Lee a paperback copy of my running book; he said he was impressed.

Public Perceptions of Depression, Mental Illness, and Violence

"The mentally ill frighten and embarrass us. And so we marginalize the people who most need our acceptance. What mental health needs is more sunlight, more candor, more unashamed conversation." - Glenn Close

Depression

In a recent U.S. national survey, over half of the people questioned did not see depression as a major health issue. In another U.S. survey, in which 25 percent of the respondents had themselves experienced depression, and another 26 percent had observed it in family members, close to half of the respondents still viewed the disorder not as a disease or a psychological problem deserving of help, but rather as a sign of personal weakness.

Mental Illness and Violence

Thanks to the media, the common public perception is that people with mental disorders are especially violence-prone.

"About 75% of films depicting a character with a serious mental illness portray that character has physically aggressive, even homicidal. Movies and television shows portraying 'psychopathic killers' and 'homicidal maniacs' have become a dime a dozen in Hollywood. Prime-time television programs depict characters with mental illness as engaging in violence about 10 times more often than other characters, and 10 to 20 times more often than the average person. ... Not surprisingly, surveys reveal that the close link between mental illness and violence in the popular media is paralleled in the minds of the general public. One survey demonstrated that about 80% of Americans believe that mentally ill people are prone to violence. This perception of heightened risk holds across a broad range of disorders, including alcoholism, cocaine dependence, schizophrenia, and even depression. In addition, between 1950 and 1996, the proportion of American adults who perceived the mentally ill as violent increased substantially. This increase is ironic, because research suggests that the percentage of murders committed by the mentally ill has declined over the past four decades."[7]

Most experts agree that incidents of violence by the mentally ill are a statistical rarity.

"In some recent studies, severely mentally ill patients without substance substance abuse disorders showed no higher risk for violence than other individuals. Furthermore, psychiatric patients who take their medication regularly aren't at elevated risk for violence compared with members of the general population. ...Still, the best estimates suggest that 90% or more of people with serious mental illness, including schizophrenia, never commit violent acts. Moreover, severe mental illness probably accounts for only about 3--5% of all violent crimes. In fact, people with schizophrenia and other severe mental disorders are far more likely to be victims than perpetrators of violence, probably because their weakened mental capacity renders them vulnerable to attacks by others. Furthermore, most major mental disorders, including major depression and anxiety disorders (such as phobias and obsessive-compulsive disorder), aren't associated with a heightened risk of physical aggression."[8]

---

[7] 50 Great Myths of Popular Psychology: Shattering Widespread Misconceptions about Human Behavior by Scott O. Lilienfeld, Steven Jay Lynn, John Ruscio, and Barry L Beyerstein

[8] 50 Great Myths of Popular Psychology: Shattering Widespread

"There's some evidence that patients with 'command hallucinations'--hearing voices instructing a person to commit an act like a murder--are at heightened risk for violence."[9]

But many experts believe that these infractions are not easily predicted or prevented; their relative infrequency makes it difficult to create a profile of individuals prone to such behavior. Individuals diagnosed with mental illness often engage in disturbing behavior without ever committing violent acts.

While there may, in many cases, have been warning signs before the actual violence, they are often clearer in hindsight. Researchers have concluded that there is a statistically significant association between mental illness and violence: Overall, the mentally ill are more likely to act out violently than the general public, but the association is weak. The overwhelming majority of people with diagnosed mental disorders do not engage in violence. Also, the manner in which mental illness contributes to violence, when it does, varies considerably and is often unclear.

Certain factors that appear to be associated

Misconceptions about Human Behavior by Scott O. Lilienfeld, Steven Jay Lynn, John Ruscio, and Barry L Beyerstein

[9] 50 Great Myths of Popular Psychology: Shattering Widespread Misconceptions about Human Behavior by Scott O. Lilienfeld, Steven Jay Lynn, John Ruscio, and Barry L Beyerstein

with an increased likelihood of violence are in line with common sense. Not surprisingly, a prior history of violence has been found to be a significant risk factor for the occurrence of future violence. So has the presence of substance abuse. Location, too, is important: The kind of neighborhood in which a mentally ill person lives appears to have a strong relationship to violence--or its absence. Moreover, violence is most likely to take place when an individual is experiencing active symptoms of a mental disorder--the low of a depressive episode, the panic of an anxiety attack--than it is while the disorder is lying dormant.

I Dream of Revenge

Therapy session: 13 September 2014

In today's session I talked about a recent dream that I had. The dream involved my elementary school principal; a thug of a man that I, and others, hated in our elementary-school days. In the dream I had him by the throat and threw him down the hall while shouting obscenities at him; other students stood by watching, which pleased me. (Note: In my elementary-school days the principal of my school found me in the hall after being sent out of the classroom by my teacher, grabbed me by the throat, threw me against a locker, and threatened, "I'll slap your face like your old man does.") Dr. Lee asked me how I felt (the question the general public most associates with psychiatrists) when I woke up. I responded that I felt both happy and angry. Happy because I got revenge in my dream, but angry because that's how I was feeling when I assaulted the principal.

Depression, Sleep, and Dreaming

"Merciful powers!
Restrain in me the cursed thoughts that nature
Gives way to in repose."
- William Shakespeare

An early warning sign of mental health troubles is disordered sleep. Difficulty sleeping is a primary symptom of depression. Not only does sleep become troubled long before other characteristics such as lack of interest in food, sex, social activity, and other symptoms become apparent; it is also the longest-lasting complaint of the depressed. It often trails on long after the patient's mood has improved and other hallmarks of the disorder are gone.

Depression is for many a recurring disorder, and the insomnia of depression waxes and wanes. When those who have had a depressive episode are functioning well they sleep better, but the sleep worsens prior to the appearance of another episode. This predictive power of sleep difficulties was documented by Michael Perlis in a 1997 study of formerly-depressed patients who were surveyed after they had completed interpersonal psychotherapy and had been in full remission for at least 4 weeks. Half of the sample had another episode of depression. They showed an increasing level of sleep disturbance over the five weeks preceding the onset of the new depression episode. The other half showed no sleep disturbance and did not suffer a recurrence.

When emotions evoked by a waking experience are strong, or more often were under-attended at the time they occurred, they may not be fully resolved by nighttime. That is, it may take us a while to come to terms with strong or neglected emotions. If, during the day, some event challenges a basic, habitual way in which we think about ourselves, it may be a threat to our self-concepts. It will probably be brushed off at the time, but the event along with its emotional baggage will be carried forward in our minds into sleep.

One theory about the purpose of dreaming (known as the regulatory function of dreams theory) is that dreaming modulates disturbances in emotion, regulating those that are troublesome. In this way, dreaming diffuses the emotional charge of the event and so prepares the sleeper to wake ready to see things in a more positive light, to make a fresh start. This does not always happen in a single night; sometimes a big reorganization of the emotional perspective of our self-concept must be made, and this may take many nights.

Among those whose low mood qualifies as major depression, some do and some do not regulate negative dreams within the night; those who do not, wake without any improvement in the gloomy way they perceive the world and their place in it (high-functioning people with little ongoing negative mood before sleep have mostly pleasant dreams and wake up in a good mood).

Differences between the dreams of the not recovered and the recovered are easy to recognize. Those recovering experience much longer, more dramatic dreams, with complex plots and changes of scene. They include more characters. They both include images drawn from older memories mixed with current issues. Both express how they feel. The recovering appear to work out their negative feelings in their dream scenarios, but the non-recovering do not.

The non-recovering express neither emotion in their dreams nor any complex blending of present images with past memories. In mild depression, dreams express emotions that have become flat, and a dreamed self that is passive and lacking responsiveness, and in severe depression, dreaming is often devoid of any coherent narrative thread.

Horse to Water

Therapy session: 20 September 2014

I didn't have a topic for today's session so I gave Dr. Lee an update on my life, the noteworthy part being some recent bad news in both my sister's and father's lives. I heard from my younger sister that my older sister and her husband had another fight and that this one included my sister hitting her husband. They plan to once again separate (next month).

There was also recent violence in my father's unmarriage. His unwife assaulted him after he insulted her. I discussed these events and my feelings about them with Dr. Lee and I decided to change my way of relating to my older sister and father. Although I believe my older sister and father need counseling to sort through their problems, I've decided not to recommend counseling to them anymore unless they bring up the topic. Using my analogy, Dr. Lee said that, "You brought the horse to water, it's up to the horse to drink." I agreed.

The Undivorced

"It takes two to destroy a marriage." -
Margaret Trudeau

The "undivorced" are husbands and wives
who stay married, but live apart or drift into
extra-marital relationships. Reasons for this new
phenomenon vary and include economic
pressures, including fear of losing a spouse's
health insurance, religious beliefs, and lack of
patience for lawyers and red tape, and the
avoidance of custody battles where children are
involved. Therapists tend to agree that having
undivorced parents is confusing for children. But
even adults find the arrangement can be an
emotional challenge.

Psychiatrist and marriage therapist Scott
Haltzman said: "At first glance, it appears that
being undivorced is the best of all possible
worlds. Nonetheless, in my clinical experience it
is just the opposite. It provides very little gain
and can be quite detrimental to the status of the
individuals involved. It inhibits your capacity to
proceed with healthy relationships with other
people. Exactly what do you say to somebody
with whom you are romantically attracted when
you are not exactly married, but not divorced?"[10]

---

[10]   Psychology Today magazine article by Rita Watson

Depression and Divorce

Depression that affects one partner has an effect on the other partner, the relationship and ultimately the entire family. Depression often leads couples to seek counseling, fearful the depression will lead to divorce. The depression itself doesn't lead directly to divorce. Rather, it is the consequences of not addressing the depression. Depression can lead to other problems, such as marital infidelity, which can cause a divorce. Affairs aren't the only problems. Often, one partner gets so depressed that he stops working, and that can lead to a cascade of other problems. The other partner feels compelled to pick up the slack, especially if there are children. They may be understanding and sympathetic at first, but as exhaustion and frustration increase, the feelings of the non-depressed partner may turn to anger or resentment. Also, if the depressed partner doesn't enjoy engaging in activities the couple used to do together, that can be another source of irritation. If the depression persists for months or years, both partners can feel the distance between them widening.

In one study on treating depression, Italian researchers reviewed the data on whether couple therapy was a better way than individual therapy to treat depression in one partner and found no difference between couple therapy and individual therapy on the symptoms of depression. But couple therapy better reduced relationship distress, they reported in the journal Psychiatric Quarterly. Often, talking about the depression, whether alone or with a partner in therapy, brings up other issues in a marriage that, when addressed, help ease the depression. The couples most likely to stay together are those who acknowledge the depression as a problem, try to relieve it, and keep talking with each other.

The Gentle Hum of Anxiety

Therapy session: 4 October 2014

I started today's session giving Dr. Lee an update on recent events in my life. One of these events was the ending of my procrastination about starting the application process for my wife's spousal visa for our move to Canada. Our future move to Canada is a source of anxiety for me. I talked about the move and why it's causing me anxiety, mostly financial worries. I said that I've had financial worries for a long time, and that I probably inherited them from my parents. I recalled being worried all throughout university about my future job prospects (more than once I contemplated switching majors and universities, and I did a minor in computer science to improve my marketability).

Depression and Anxiety

"To reduce your worry, you must assume that what you fear may happen is certainly going to happen." - Seneca

According to clinical psychologist Dr. Leon F. Seltzer, the most common type of depressed person therapists encounter suffers from what's frequently called "agitated depression" (also called "anxious depression"). Such a distraught state is made up of roughly equal amounts of anxiety and depression. There are many links between these two distressful emotions and moods.

Some researchers, aware of their fundamental similarities, have even conjectured that anxiety and depression may both be facets of yet another disorder, as yet not clearly identified. Just as a person can ponder her way into the depths of depression by telling herself that her situation is hopeless, she can think herself into anxiety by assessing her situation as precariously out of control. What defines individuals as anxious is that they feel threatened by people and circumstances that most people would take in stride. Experiencing fear—or even panic—with (objectively, at least) little provocation. They live lives of chronic worry, insecurity, and a truly frightening sense of vulnerability. Tense, nervous, and hyper-vigilant (whether about a specific situation or just in general), it's difficult for them to relax.

Since strong emotions affect our body just as much as our mind (which triggers them in the first place), the physical symptoms of anxiety can be every bit as disturbing as the emotion itself.

Ultimately, the person's level of anxiety determines the severity of his symptoms. But if you've ever had a powerful anxiety, or worse, panic, attack, you've probably experienced increased muscle tension and rigidity, an accelerated heart rate or palpitations, light-headedness, chest pain, shortness of breath, a dry mouth, trembling, sweating and clammy hands, a queasy stomach, nausea, and perhaps even diarrhea.

Behaviorally, your anxiety would have manifested itself through a pronounced restlessness, likely characterized by squirming and fidgeting; and you might have felt compelled to pace the floor, stamp your feet, clench your hands, grind your teeth, or some other kind of edgy, jittery action. Moreover, your feelings of apprehension or distress might have included a sense of being critically watched (and so making a terrible fool of yourself), a surreal perception of self-detachment or unreality (technically referred to as "depersonalization" or "derealization"), a fear of dying or impending doom, or even a sense of going crazy. Along with these most disconcerting feelings, you may experience yourself as uptight, dissociated, "flipped out," uncomfortably "energized" (because of the adrenalin surge accompanying your anxiety), or – at worst – terrified.

Here is a 4-step plan for dealing with a panic

attack:

1. Acknowledge the panic symptoms. As previously stated, thought suppression–telling yourself to stop thinking something–does not work. A preferred response is to recognize the uncomfortable feelings and remind yourself that you're not in danger: "This is just a panic attack. Although it's scary and overwhelming, I'm not in danger."

2. Stay in the situation. This step is especially challenging since one of the symptoms of panic is feeling like you're going crazy. Because your brain's amygdala (the area which controls the fear response) sends rapid fire signals preparing you to fight or flee, you'll need to counteract these irrational impulses. Grounding strategies include feeling your feet on the ground, or your hands on the steering wheel, or bracing yourself against a wall. Try to stay in the situation until your rational mind returns.

3. Be present. When you have a panic attack you are not living in the present. You're reacting to a past action, or to an imagined future event. Being mindful will help you take action to calm yourself down.

4. Take action. Now that your mind and body are calmer, it's time to do one or more of the

following actions:

- Count to 10.
- Breathe slowly and deeply.
- Close your eyes to block out overwhelming stimulation.
- Challenge unhealthy thoughts (see "A Wasted Session").

Repeat steps 1-4 until the attack ceases.

If these relaxation techniques don't work for you, you may want to consider medication. Medications can help reduce symptoms associated with panic attacks as well as depression. Several types of medication have been shown to be effective in managing symptoms of panic attacks, including:

- Benzodiazepines. If you seek care in an emergency room for symptoms of a panic attack, you will likely be given a benzodiazepine to help stop the attack. These mild sedatives belong to a group of medicines called central nervous system depressants. Benzodiazepines may be habit-forming (causing mental or physical dependence), especially when taken for a long time or in high doses. Benzodiazepines approved by the U.S. Food and Drug Administration (FDA) for the treatment of panic disorder include alprazolam (Niravam, Xanax), clonazepam (Klonopin) and lorazepam (Ativan).

- Selective serotonin reuptake inhibitors (SSRIs). Generally safe with a low risk of serious side effects, SSRI antidepressants are typically recommended as the first choice of medications to treat panic attacks. SSRIs approved by the FDA for the treatment of panic disorder include fluoxetine (Prozac), paroxetine (Paxil, Pexeva) and sertraline (Zoloft).

- Serotonin and norepinephrine reuptake inhibitors (SNRIs). These medications are another class of antidepressants. The SNRI drug called venlafaxine hydrochloride (Effexor XR) is FDA approved for the treatment of panic disorder.

Ruminating About Rumination

Therapy session: 11 October 2014

I'm unhappy about my university experience. It was a difficult time for me, and I experienced little success, both academically and socially. I blame depression for this. I often ruminate about this period because I believe it could have been a much better time in my life. During this session I talked about some failed interactions with the opposite sex that I had during this period.

One, in particular, with a girl I tutored in physics. She was an attractive girl who I would normally have asked out on dates (after ending the tutoring) had she not had one glaring flaw: an anger problem. I don't think she knew she had an anger problem but I spotted it. I come from a family where anger is a problem, and I believe I can recognize anger problems in others. She was the second-angriest female I've met (the angriest was a girl I met in high school who used to pick fights with other girls and assault her tough boyfriend).

After the session I did a depression checklist;

I scored 14/45, which puts me in the mild degree of anxiety category (11-20). That's an improvement from my score in 21-30 range (moderate anxiety) before starting therapy. My goal is to get my score in the 0-4 range (minimal anxiety).

Rumination

"Wild beasts run away from dangers when they see them. Once they have escaped, they are free of anxiety. But we are tormented by both the future and the past." - Seneca

Rumination entails thinking repeatedly about one's shortcomings and mistakes. It is a self-focused, self-critical frame of mind that is also known as "brooding." Unlike worry, which is focused on the future, rumination is focused on the past. When we ruminate, we become fruitlessly occupied with the fact that we are unhappy and with the causes, meanings, and consequences of our unhappiness. Similarly to worrying, rumination gives the person the illusion that it can help him understand himself better: "If I keep re-hashing my disappointing time in university, I will be able to understand why I'm depressed." However, when a person becomes fixated with finding every single thing that is wrong with him, it becomes difficult to take proactive action. Studies on rumination show: the more a person ruminates, the less likely he is to take action to modify those things he doesn't like about himself (Nolen-Hoeksema et al., 2000). Over two decades of research on rumination links it with the development and maintenance of depressive disorders. Rumination perpetuates negative mood, particularly in individuals prone to depression. They become stuck in a vicious cycle of negativity.

One tactic I found useful to overcome this cycle of rumination was rephrasing my thoughts. For example, I'd like to leave my current company, but I haven't been able to find a better job. Thinking "I'm stuck in this job" has depressed me in the past. These days whenever I have that thought I replace it with "I choose to stay in this job." It's a small change in thinking but it makes a difference. When I stay in a situation by choice, I recognize that I have some control and therefore feel less helpless. "I choose to stay in this job," is a statement of some power. However, it is important to not just say "I choose" but to really choose to do the thing that you are unhappy about. (I am consciously choosing to stay in this job, and could leave if I decided to.)

Another application of this tactic is "I don't like this job but I will do it until I get something better." I don't have to like the situation; I am allowed to feel bad about it. But the thought is affirmative and has some power. My choice is made from free will. It is a mobilizer, spurring problem-solving and making decisions about difficult situations. My last application of this tactic is turning "I can't" into "I won't." I change, for example, "I can't look for a job" to "I won't look for a job." I say the substituted thought out loud. The point of saying it out loud is to create a feeling of power and choice. Changing the language of thoughts is mobilizing, because the brain believes thoughts. The feelings of power and choice are good counterweights to the drag of negative and hopeless thinking.

Nothing Matters but the Weekend

Weekend Activity Scheduling and Monitoring

Strangely, weekends are the most difficult time of the week for me. When nothing is planned for my weekends, I often revert to my old habit of napping. I decided to try a CBT activity called activity scheduling. I made the following to-do list of activities that I could do on weekends ranked by difficulty and predicted pleasure.

Activity	Difficulty (easy, medium, hard)	Pleasure Prediction Rating (0-100%)
Chores		
1. Vacuum a room.	Easy	60
2. Floss teeth.	"	70
3. Meditate.	"	70
4. Fill out spousal visa form.	"	60

5. Put recyclables out.	"	70
6. Clean bathroom mirror.	"	70
7. Clean playroom with son.	"	70
8. Tidy an area.	"	50
9. Shower and shave.	"	70
10. Take a picture of guitar (for ad).	"	70
11. Apply cream to dry areas of body.	"	60
12. Clean air filter machine	"	60
13. Wash dishes.	Medium	40
14. Do a wash.	"	40
Pleasurable activities		
1. Watch a TV episode.		80
2. Read a book.		80
3. Go to park		70

with son.		
4. Phone friend or family member.		60

Here is what I actually did on one of those days:

Time	Activity	Pleasure Rating (0-100%)
8:00-9:00	Sleep	
9:00-10:00	Cleaned mirrors.	80--Easy and good to do.
10:00-11:00	Phoned friend.	70--Enjoyable.
11:00-12:00	Went to park with son.	80--Easy and weather was nice.
12:00-1:00	"	
1:00-2:00	Read a book	80--Enjoyable and satisfying to finish book.
2:00-3:00	Lunch	
3:00-4:00	Nap	

4:00-5:00	"	
5:00-6:00	"	
6:00-7:00	Filled out visa forms.	70--Not hard and felt good to do.
7:00-8:00	Applied cream to dry parts of body.	70--Easy and felt good.
8:00-9:00	Ate dinner and cleaned up.	
9:00-10:00	Watched TV episode.	80
10:00-11:00	Shower/Sleep	
11:00-12:00	Sleep	

As you can see, I still relapsed into my old habit of napping, but I was able to minimize the nap. On other weekends I slept more, accomplished less, and felt lousy, so this day was an improvement. I also don't think it's bad to take a midday nap on the weekend; my problem is that I do too much of it. Overall, I was happy with this day, and the above CBT exercise helped make it happen.

Dosage Adjustment

I've been on Prozac for years, and decided recently to lower my dose from 20 mg to 10 mg per day after reading the following in Dr. David Burns' book *Feeling Good: The New Mood Therapy:*

"SSRIs are often prescribed in doses that are unnecessarily high. Because they have so few side effects, doctors feel comfortable prescribing high doses and may prescribe more than is really needed. For example, although 20 mg to 80 mg per day was the dose range initially recommended for Prozac, a single dose of 10 mg per day will be sufficient for many patients. Once they are feeling better, many patients need only 5 mg per day, or even less. These smaller doses are much less expensive and will produce fewer side effects. These low doses are effective because Prozac stays in the body for a much longer period of time than most other drugs--as long as several weeks. When you take Prozac, your blood level continues to increase each day because the Prozac leaves your body so slowly. After a while your blood level becomes quite high. This is why you may need only a tiny dose if you have been taking Prozac for several weeks or more."

The Effectiveness of Therapy

Therapy session: 1 November 2014

I started today's session by talking about Prozac. Specifically, I asked Dr. Lee if it was still under patent protection. (I should probably know this since I've been working at intellectual property law firms for over seven years.) I didn't think it was and Dr. Lee confirmed that it wasn't. I asked because I recently had the thought, "If generic Prozac is available, why am I taking the costly regular Prozac?"

My grandmother was a pharmacist, and often advised me to buy generics when available, saying they are the same drug but much cheaper. Dr. Lee said that Korean doctors still prescribe regular Prozac because they believe there is a difference between regular (patented) drugs and generic ones; they believe the regular versions are better. I don't think that any difference is worth the increased cost so I told him that for my next prescription refill I'd like to try generic Prozac. He responded that that was fine and made a note on his computer.

He then asked me how I felt about the doctors

for not prescribing generic Prozac. I responded that I think it irritated me. This led to a discussion of my feelings about him. I said that after earlier sessions I was unhappy about the lack of analysis I was getting from him. I said that I had the thought, "Why am I going to this guy every Saturday morning when I could just talk to a friend or family member for 45 minutes once a week and get the same result?" He asked me if I now saw the difference. I responded that I had, and said something similar to: A friend or family member likely wouldn't listen as well, would provide unnecessary or unhelpful advice, and wouldn't understand, to name just a few problems.

The Effectiveness of Psychotherapy

"If we hope for more significant therapeutic change, we must encourage our patients to assume responsibility--that is, to apprehend how they themselves contribute to their distress." - *Irvin D. Yalom*

Studies show that most people suffering from emotional disturbance who have at least several sessions of psychotherapy are better off than untreated individuals. And 50 percent of patients noticeably improved after eight therapy sessions, while 75 percent of individuals in psychotherapy progressed by the end of six months (American

Psychological Association, How to Find Help Through Psychotherapy, 1998). Research suggests that psychotherapy is frequently at least as effective as medication, and that the benefits last longer. Other scientific studies support a combination of psychotherapy and psycho-pharmacology as the most effective treatment for serious depression and other debilitating mental disorders.

To assess the effectiveness of your therapy, consider these questions: Do you leave each session feeling that your time and money have been well-spent?

One way to assess the value of any particular session is to look back on it in order to articulate what you accomplished. What was your take-home? What about your therapy is working well for you? Many therapists end each session with a session summary. If your therapist does not routinely review the session at the end, consider requesting a summary. Starting your review with five to ten minutes left will give you time to consolidate and reinforce what you have gained. It's helpful also to look by the end of the session at any unfinished pieces that you will want to explore further next session, and to tell your therapist of anything in the session that did not work for you.

How far do you think you have come in

solving your problems?

If you think of therapy as a journey, how far are you along that journey? If your progress thus far is unclear to you, ask your therapist to share her view.

If your therapy sessions aren't going as well as you'd like, here are some ideas to help you choose a session focus:

- Digest and learn from a specific upsetting interaction that happened the prior week.
- Make a plan of action to prepare for a challenge that you see ahead.
- Ease a negative feeling you have been experiencing such as anxiety, anger or depression.
- Improve a relationship at home or at work.
- Understand how experiences earlier in your life have been affecting how you handle situations that you are facing now.
- Understand the source and remove a self-defeating belief (e.g., "I can't possibly succeed.").
- Understand the origin and remove a self-defeating habit (e.g., eating excessively or quickness to anger).

Rumination Redux

"My life has been full of terrible misfortunes, most of which never happened." - Michel de Montaigne

I decided to track my ruminative thoughts for a week; the results are tabulated below. I carried a pocket-sized notebook and a pen with me at all times for this week, and recorded instances of ruminative thoughts that I noticed.

Date (Nov.):	3	4	5	6	7	8	9
Number of Ruminative Thoughts:	12	3	2	2	4	3	2

Note: Negative thoughts are insidious, so I've likely under-reported the number of ruminative thoughts, but the general trend remains unchanged.

An important observation about the data of

the above table is that the number of ruminative thoughts decreases dramatically just by paying attention to them. (Note the drop of 12 ruminative thoughts to 3 ruminative thoughts from 11/3 to 11/4.) I also noticed that I felt a little better during this period. Mindfulness helps.

Depressives often relive remembered emotions or pre-live anticipated ones. When they do this they remove themselves from reality, and suffer the agonies of events that are either long past or may never happen. They end up feeling worse as a result.

Living in the moment and treating your thoughts and emotions as passing messages similar to sounds, sights, tastes, and touch keeps them from drowning out the signals your senses deliver–signals that can keep you off the road to rumination.

Five steps for practicing mindfulness throughout the day:

- When possible do just one thing at a time.
- Pay full attention to what you are doing.
- When the mind wanders from what you are doing, bring it back.
- Repeat step three many times.
- Investigate your distractions.

Emotional Health

Therapy session: 22 November 2014

I realized after today's session that the greatest benefit that my therapy with Dr. Lee has provided is improvement of my marriage. This therapy has helped me find solutions to some of my marital problems, and avoid other problems. Today I talked again about marital issues; particularly, about some frustrations I have with my wife. I think the biggest of which is that at times I find my wife difficult to deal with; I find her emotional intensity to be overwhelming at times.

Emotional Health

"Dishonoring what we feel is an epidemic that has us self-medicating as a culture and trying to numb ourselves." - Abiola Abrams

What does it mean to be emotionally healthy?
It means that you are comfortable in your skin. You do not wish you could be someone else, nor do you look down on others for not

being like you. You know what you are thinking and feeling, even if sometimes that means knowing that you don't know. You have your own consistent ethical code which enables you to distinguish right from wrong. You are stoical in the face of adversity, realistic in your ideas, and wise in your judgments. You have the capacity for insight into your actions. You are a good judge of what others are thinking and feeling. You are adaptable without losing yourself. You believe that life is to be enjoyed, not endured.

In developed nations, emotional health is linked to our life experiences, and there are four main experiences that lead to emotional health in adulthood. The first is being loved in your early years, and wisely nurtured subsequently. The second is receiving the right kind of supportive, loving assistance in the wake of childhood adversity. The third is to be prompted by a shock in adulthood to undertake a complete rethink of life, resulting in a sudden appreciation of life. The last is a profound spiritual or therapeutic experience.

Depression is a disorder of impaired emotion regulation. More so than mentally healthy individuals, depressives have difficulty with unpleasant emotions. Unpleasant emotions are invariably accompanied by sensations and feelings in the body.

"Psychologist Steve Hayes and his colleagues concluded from a review of more than one hundred research studies that many forms of emotional disturbance are the result of unhealthy efforts to escape and avoid emotions--that is, the result of experiential avoidance."[11]

When we try to ignore bodily sensations, thoughts, and feelings that are part of our emotional experience, our "psychological engines" usually seize up. Rather than seeing them as bad and threatening, a view that triggers avoidance and gets us stuck in suffering, we should try to see unpleasant emotions for what they are: passing mental events. We should try to greet them with a sense of interest and curiosity, rather than with a sense of unease, hatred, and dread. We should welcome them in, as they are already here anyway. This disrupts the automatic links among body sensations, feelings, and thoughts that perpetuate vicious cycles and downward mood spirals.

---

[11] The Mindful Way Through Depression: Freeing Yourself From Chronic Unhappiness by Mark Williams, John Teasdale, Zindel Segal, and Jon Kabat-Zinn

Applied Philosophy

Therapy session: 6 December 2014

Once again, I had no topic for today's session, so I had to free associate. I talked about the application of philosophy to mental health problems. I dabbled in philosophy in university, and while doing some self-help for my depression after graduation I wondered why there weren't philosophers treating the mentally ill. As I saw it, mental illness is just distorted thinking, and thinking is philosophy's realm.

People with depression often blame external factors for their bad moods. They blame the past, their parents (my scapegoat), their coworkers, the economy, politics, etc. They deny responsibility for their beliefs and feelings. This makes them feel more helpless, frantic, and depressed.

Stoicism

"The robber of your free will does not exist."
- Epictetus

Ancient Greek philosophy is a form of psychological therapy. Most ancient philosophies equate the good in life with what is good for us, beneficial or helpful, in the sense of contributing to our fundamental health and well-being, not physically but mentally and morally, in terms of our character.

Our modern notion of self-help was an integral part of Stoic ethics. These were presented as a form of medicine or therapy for the mind by ancient authors. For the Stoic philosophers, the only thing of any ultimate importance in life was virtue, particularly wisdom, and extrinsic things were of absolutely secondary value, because they were unimportant when it came to attaining happiness and freedom from emotional suffering.

The Greek Stoic philosopher Epictetus (A.D. 55–155) believed that "some things are up to us, and others are not." He believed that a person's body, property, reputation, job, parents, friends, coworkers, boss, past, future, mortality, the weather and the economy were not within her control (zone 1)*. But he also believed that a person's thoughts were within her control (zone 2). A lot of suffering arises, Epictetus argued, because people make two mistakes.

First, they try to exert complete control over something in zone 1. Then, when they fail to control it, they feel helpless, frantic, angry, guilty, anxious, or depressed. Second, they don't take responsibility for zone 2–their thoughts, which are under their control. Instead, they blame external factors for their thoughts and end up feeling bitter, helpless, victimized, and at the mercy of external circumstances. Stoic philosophers like Epictetus insisted that no one can ever force us to believe something against our will. No one can brainwash us if we know how to resist them. We always have a choice what to think and believe.

The earliest Stoic writings define the "passions" they sought to overcome as consisting of irrational, excessive and unhealthy forms of fear and desire. They are said to be "unnatural" in the sense of harming our natural pursuit of fulfillment in life. The virtue of a wise person consists in her ability to endure painful feelings and rise above them, while continuing to maintain his relationships and interaction with the world, to care sufficiently about ourselves and others but not enough to anxiously worry. A wise person conquers his passions by becoming stronger than them, not by eliminating all traces of emotion from his life. The Stoic ideal is not to be passionless in the sense of being apathetic, hardhearted, or insensitive. Rather, it is to experience natural affection for ourselves, our loved ones, and others, and to value our lives in accord with nature, which open us up to experiencing certain natural emotional reactions to loss or frustration.

*Some of the things in zone 1 are, of course, partially under a person's control.

Get Yourself to the Ancient Greeks

Therapy session: 20 December 2014

"Vex not thy spirit at the course of things, they heed not thy vexations." - *Marcus Aurelius*

In today's session I talked again about Stoicism. Epictetus' technique of defining the limits of our control, which I described previously, is particularly useful when thinking about the times when we were children or adolescents, because during that period we were very much at the mercy of circumstances and of other people–particularly our parents. As I've stated earlier, rumination is a serious problem for me; it contributes to my cycle of depression. It helps when I remind myself not to blame myself for things that happened in my youth that were outside of my control.

Therapy session: 27 December 2014

In today's session I talked about a change of my thinking that occurred during the past week.

One thought process that has fueled my depression is what Dr. Lee calls my "give-and-take relationship philosophy." I believe that relationships are a two-way street, and that contact (e-mail, phone calls, gifting, etc.) should be reciprocated. I get annoyed and sometimes angry when there is a lack of reciprocation. I tend to respond to a lack of reciprocation by withdrawing from the relationship, which increases my loneliness, thus contributing to my depression. However, a piece of Stoic philosophy has caused a change in my thinking. Stoics believed that it was more important to love than to be loved:

"The Stoic loves other people in a very free, giving way. His love is not at all conditional upon its being reciprocated by the person loved. The Stoic does not compromise his own moral integrity or mental serenity in his love for others nor is his love impaired by his knowledge of the mortality of his loved ones. Rather, the Stoic's love and natural affection are tempered by reason. His love and affection serve only to enrich his humanity, never to subject him to psychic torment."

Loneliness

"What should young people do with their lives

today? Many things, obviously. But the most daring thing is to create stable communities in which the terrible disease of loneliness can be cured." - Kurt Vonnegut

A lack of close friends and a dearth of broader social contact generally bring the emotional discomfort or distress known as loneliness. It begins with an awareness of a deficiency of relationships. This awareness plays through our brain with an emotional soundtrack. It makes us sad and empty, and fills us with a longing for contact. We feel isolated, distanced from others, and deprived. These feelings tear away at our emotional well-being.

Despite the negative effects of loneliness, it is a normal feeling. Everyone feels lonely sometimes–after a break-up with a friend or lover, when we move to a new place, and when we are excluded from a social gathering. But chronic loneliness is something else entirely. It is a sign of maladjustment. Lonely individuals report higher levels of perceived stress even when exposed to the same stressors as non-lonely people, and even when they are relaxing. The social interaction lonely people have is not as positive as those of other people, hence the relationships they have do not buffer them from stress as relationships normally do.

Loneliness destroys the quality and efficiency of sleep, so that it is less restorative, both physically and psychologically. The lonely wake up more at night and spend less time in bed actually sleeping than do the non-lonely. But the worst effects of chronic loneliness are that it is a major cause of depression and alcoholism, and it increases the risk of suicide.

To escape loneliness, extend yourself. Start small; don't focus on trying to find the love of your life or to reinvent yourself all at once. Try to get small doses of the positive sensations that come from positive social interactions. To accomplish this, you need a safe place to experiment.

To improve your odds of eliciting a positive reaction, and to reduce your odds of being disappointed, you may want to confine your experimental outreach to the safer confines of charitable activities. Volunteer at a shelter or a hospice, teach elders how to use computers, tutor children, read to the blind, or help with a kids' sports team. There will be no big scene of fulfillment, but you may begin to feel the positive sensations that can reinforce your desire to change, while building your confidence, and improving your ability to self-regulate. Even small talk, when it is welcomed and shared, can be a co-regulating, calming device, and the positive change it can bring to your body chemistry can help you get beyond the fearful outlook that holds you back.

The solution to loneliness is not a high

quantity of, but a high quality of relationships. Human connections have to be meaningful and satisfying for each of the people involved, and not according to some external measure. Moreover, relationships are necessarily mutual and require fairly similar levels of intimacy and intensity on both sides. Even casual conversation needs to proceed at a pace that is comfortable for both. Coming on too strong, oblivious to the other person's response, is likely to push someone away. So part of selection is sensing which prospective relationships are promising, and which are not. Loneliness makes us attentive to social signals. The trick is to be sufficiently calm in order to interpret those signals accurately.

We are built for social contact. Social interaction is crucial for our mental health, and there are serious, life-threatening consequences when we don't get enough of it.

A Fear of Poverty

Therapy session: 3 January 2015

"The prevalent fear of poverty among the educated classes is the worst moral disease from which our civilization suffers." - William James

During my reading of philosophy this week I came upon the term "fear of poverty." I think it was the first time I've encountered the idea. I told Dr. Lee that I think I have a fear of poverty. He said that maybe I fear ending up back in the trailer park. (I lived in a trailer park until I was about 10 years old.) I agreed. I spent the remainder of the session talking about this fear. I said that I think this fear has caused me to procrastinate about dealing with my financial issue. This procrastination causes anxiety which feeds my depression. I also said that I think I'd feel better if I took action on my financial issue. My plan for the upcoming week is to take action on this issue.

Therapy session: 10 January 2015

"To reduce your worry, you must assume that what you fear may happen is certainly going to happen."- Seneca

During this week I took action about my financial issue. I didn't feel as good afterward as I thought I would. I told Dr. Lee that my expectations were probably unrealistic; it's not realistic to take a small action on a long unresolved issue and expect to feel significantly better. Dr. Lee responded that my thinking shows my strong desire to get better.

For the rest of the session I talked about my worries about moving to Canada with my family (a topic I've discussed before). At the end of the session Dr. Lee suggested that I share my feelings with my wife about our future move to Canada. I agreed with the suggestion, but realized after the session that I'd already done that once. I thought it might be better to devise a plan for the move and coping plans in case we experience difficulties. Maybe it would be best to do both.

Peniaphobia

The fear of poverty is known as "peniaphobia," which is a combination of the

Greek words penia, meaning poverty, and, phobia, meaning fear. Phobias arise from a combination of external events (i.e., traumatic events) and internal predispositions (i.e., genetics). Many specific phobias can be traced back to a specific triggering event, usually a traumatic experience at an early age.

It is believed that heredity and brain chemistry combine with life experiences to produce phobias. The best way to deal with a fear is to confront it. Assume that what you fear may happen will happen, and develop a coping plan. As an example, I fear that when I return to Canada I will not be able to find a job and will not be able to support my family and that they will suffer. To deal with this fear I assume that I won't be able to find a job in Canada, and ask myself, "How will I cope with unemployment?"

I answer that my wife and I have savings so we will be fine for at least a year, I can probably easily find part-time employment, and it will give me time to complete and publish another book. Having this coping plan makes me feel better.

If you need to talk to someone about your fear, talk with positive people who have overcome their fears. Don't talk about your fear with negative people, some of whom may be family members. Most negative people haven't overcome their own fears and will likely make yours worse. Once you examine your fear, you can take action to minimize its effects.

All Mediocre Therapies Must Come to an End

Therapy session: 17 January 2015

I have about one month of therapy left (Dr. Lee will stop practicing at my current hospital)–a good time to do another depression checklist. I scored 9/45, which puts me in the borderline degree of anxiety category (5-10). That's a 5-point improvement from my score of 14/45 (mild anxiety) of October 11, 2014. I'm happy about my progress. However, it looks unlikely that I'll achieve my goal of a score in the 0-5 range by the end of this therapy.

I am relieved that this therapy is ending, though. Dr. Lee is young and seems to be an inexperienced psychiatrist, and I've wanted to switch therapists for a while. The lack of options has kept me from doing so. After this therapy ends, I plan to continue taking Prozac and do CBT exercises on my own until I find a good, affordable therapist to see me to the finishing line of my therapeutic journey.

Looking back at this therapy, one aspect that I'm unhappy with was the lack of preparation about the process I was provided with by Dr. Lee. In fairness, the same criticism applies to the two other therapeutic relationships I had in Canada. I've had numerous unanswered questions in my head about the process that have added to my anxiety. I've felt like a child who couldn't swim and was pushed into the water by lifeguards to figure out how. Research supports my criticism:

"A persuasive body of psychotherapy research demonstrates that the therapist should carefully prepare new patients by informing them about psychotherapy--its basic assumptions, rationale, and what each client can do to maximize his or her own progress. Patients are already burdened with the primary anxiety that brings them to therapy and it makes little sense to plunge them into a process that may create secondary anxiety--anxiety from exposure to an ambiguous social situation without guidelines for proper behavior or participation. Therefore it is wise to prepare patients systematically for the process of psychotherapy. Preparation for individual psychotherapy is also essential. Though individuals are likely to have had experience with intense relationships, it is highly unlikely that they have been in a relationship requiring them to trust fully, to reveal all, to hold nothing back, to examine all nuances of their feelings to another, and to receive nonjudgmental acceptance. In initial interviews it is important to cover ground rules, including confidentiality, the necessity for full disclosure, the importance of dreams, and the need for patience.[12]"

Another complaint I have about this therapy is Dr. Lee's lack of engagement. I found him to be too distant, uninvolved, unsupportive, and impersonal. This is another common complaint about therapists.

---

[12] The Gift of Therapy by Irvin D. Yalom

Voices From the Past

Therapy session: 24 January 2015

As previously stated, therapy can be used to understand how experiences early in life are affecting how you handle situations now. I realized in today's session that the abuse I experienced from my parents is causing conflict between my wife and me. I talked about a fight I had with my wife this week when I intervened in a conflict between her and our son.

As I've done before, I criticized her handling of the situation in front of my son. This criticism angered my wife, and caused the argument. (I apologized the next morning.) Dr. Lee helped me realize that her behavior reminds me of abuse I experienced in the past, and causes me to get angry with her. I say to myself that her parental skills are poor, and that she is handling the situation badly but subconsciously I am trying to protect my son from perceived abuse.

How the Past Can Be Changed

"The past isn't dead; it isn't even past." - William Faulkner

The events of the past exist nowhere else but in our memories, which give rise to the feelings and thoughts we have about them. By themselves, events are neutral. We place judgments on them based on how they affected us, rendering good judgments about those things which benefited us and bad judgments about those things which harmed us. It's the feelings that result from those judgments that remain with us, not the events themselves.

And though we can't change our memories of events, we can change whether they harmed or benefited us. We can do this by finding a way to create value out of events we judged as harmful. If we can genuinely use past events as catalysts for growth, reinterpreting them as positive events that may have been traumatic but which actually led to our development, we can free ourselves from the pain associated with our memories of them.

How then can we break free of the past? By using it as fuel for growth in the present. If an event from our past remains painful to think about, we should understand that pain as an indication we have unfinished business–not with whoever or whatever else was involved in the event itself, but with ourselves. Maybe someone hurt us. Maybe we hurt someone else. Maybe we made a choice out of weakness or fear or anger that we regret.

We don't have to waste time in recriminations or in wishing we could go back in time to change what happened. We only need to find a way to turn that hurt or regret into a catalyst for growth moving forward from today. Take a good look back at your past, and see if you can find a way to think about it like that. Instead of painful traumas you'd rather not think about, you may see opportunities for growth.

Important Realizations

Therapy session: 7 February 2015

During my recent two-week therapy hiatus, I came to two important realizations. With my therapy with Dr. Lee about to end, I've been doing my own evaluation of it. A complaint I have about this therapy is that I feel I haven't gotten enough back from Dr. Lee. This is the same complaint I have about everyone in my life. I feel that, to varying degrees, my wife, my extended family, and my friends don't give me enough; don't message me enough, telephone enough, send gifts; generally, don't care enough. I told Dr. Lee this and he agreed that it's an important realization. He then asked me what I would do with this realization. I responded that I plan to stop focusing on what I get from my relationships. I thought to myself that I would try to adhere to the Stoic definition of love (detailed earlier).

The second realization I had was that I've been perceiving the therapy relationship between Dr. Lee and me incorrectly; it was always a doctor-patient relationship to me, and I was concerned about crossing doctor-patient boundaries. But therapeutic relationships aren't supposed to be doctor-patient relationships. I think this hindered my therapy. Dr. Lee mentioned that he tried to point this out to me; he said that he didn't properly explain how therapy is conducted. I won't make this mistake in my next course of therapy. After over a year of once a week sessions, Dr. Lee and I shook hands, and I walked out of Seoul National University Hospital's psychiatry department, probably never to return again.

The Therapeutic Relationship

"Suffering in silence means more suffering."- *Dinesh Bhugra*

A depressive can understand what goes wrong with relationships in her life by examining the therapeutic relationship as it is occurring. Even though the therapeutic relationship is not the same as a friendship, there is much overlap, particularly the intimate nature of the discussion. A good therapist can make observations about a depressive that might throw light on what happens between her and others.

By adhering to a doctor-patient relationship, I think I was unknowingly subscribing to the old

Freudian conception of therapy described in the following. In a 1912 paper, Freud advised doctors practicing psychoanalysis that the physician "should be opaque to his patients, and, like a mirror, show them nothing but what is shown to him."

In psychoanalysis, there is a specific rationale for this rule. The theory holds that patients tend to re-enact with therapists the relationships they had with their parents. This is called transference. By paying careful attention to this unfolding drama–as it plays out in the office–the therapist and patient can uncover and resolve childhood conflicts. If a therapist interjects information about herself, she clouds the mirror and compromises the process.

Epilogue: Relapse

"Depression is recurring and cyclic. What we have is treatments, not cures. You're never really free of it; you always have to be prepared for a recurrence and be ready to stave it off as it could creep up on you." - Andrew Solomon

Now that I've finished a book on overcoming depression, I'm going to drop a bomb on you: I don't believe depression can be cured; not with our current knowledge of human psychology. The best that can be done at the current time is to reduce its symptoms to a minimum. Being a depressive is like being a drug addict; there's always the chance of relapse.

Major depression in adults is often recurrent: half of people with first episodes will have a second episode. The current standard of care is to recommend medicine indefinitely after three or more recurrences. (These recommendations are based on evidence gathered in clinical trials of moderate-to-severe depression in adults. Many studies were short-term; few followed patients for longer than two years.)

If you have had many years of unremitting

depression or if you have been prone to many recurrent attacks of depression, you might want to consider maintenance therapy for a longer period of time. Since doctors are becoming more aware of the relapsing nature of mood disorders, the use of antidepressants on a long-term or prophylactic basis is gaining greater favor.

Some doctors routinely recommend therapy with antidepressants indefinitely, in much the same way they might insist that patients with diabetes must take daily insulin to regulate their blood sugar. Several research studies suggest that such maintenance therapy can reduce the incidence of depressive relapses.

However, research studies also indicate that treatment with the cognitive therapy techniques described in this book can also reduce depressive relapses. In addition, these studies suggest that the preventive effect of cognitive therapy may be greater than the preventive effect of antidepressant medications. One important advantage of cognitive behavioral therapy is that you learn new skills to minimize or prevent future depressions.

Here are two suggestions for those tapering off antidepressant drugs, to avoid a relapse:

- Exercise. There are a number of studies indicating that exercise has a measurable anti-depressant effect. Regular long-distance runs, for example, will put you in good moods. Personally, I find that after a run I do not worry about whatever I was worrying about before I set out. You can feel very differently in as little as half an hour. And high intensity running is not required to bring about mood changes. Moderate intensity is adequate for mood benefit. Actually, moderate rather than high-intensity running is easier to maintain over time. As you run for mood, you will be constantly reminded of the benefit you are producing. And the positive feeling appears to be a universal emotion experienced after exercise. From population-based studies to clinical trials, powerful evidence suggests that exercise can have substantial effects on mood, offering treatment effects for diagnosed depression that rival antidepressant medications.

- Spend time outdoors in the daylight. There is good evidence that the absence of light makes some vulnerable people depressed. Ordinary depression gets worse during winter when there is little daylight; doctors have to prescribe higher doses of medication at that time. Spending time in the light can ameliorate depression. There is more light outside under an overcast sky then there is in the most brightly lit room. Plus, being outdoors will make you feel part of society and increase the likelihood of social interaction, both of which are likely to elevate your mood.

You can "kill two birds with one stone," by exercising outdoors, giving your mood a boost and immunizing yourself against relapse.

Whatever treatments you use, I hope that you, your loved one or friend make it out of the dark house and stay out forever.

Afterword

Thank you for buying and reading Escaping the Dark House: A Self-Help Memoir of Depression. I hope you find the techniques within as useful and effective as I have. As you put this book into practice, if you have a success story that you'd like to share, or spot an error, please send me and e-mail at williamaaronpeters@gmail.com.

Word-of-mouth is crucial for any author to succeed. If you liked the book, please consider leaving a review; even if it's only a few sentences; it would make a big difference and would be much appreciated.

About the Author

William A. Peters is a Canadian writer living in Seoul, Korea. If you want to get an e-mail when Will's next book is released, please sign up to his new release mailing list by sending him an e-mail at: williamaaronpeters@gmail.com. Your e-mail address will never be shared and you can unsubscribe at any time.

Say Hello!

You can find Will on the Internet at www.williamapeters.com. He would love it if you dropped by. Alternatively, you can follow him on Twitter, get in touch on Facebook, or send him an e-mail at: williamaaronpeters@gmail.com.

Also by William A. Peters

William A. Peters is also the author of The Resilient Runner: Mental Toughness Training for Distance Running.

Praise for The Resilient Runner:

"This is a good little book to have as a resource for anyone who is a serious competitive runner." - Michelle Williams (Goodreads reviewer)

"This was an excellent read. It was not a typical 'how to become a better runner' book." - Kristie Layne *(Goodreads reviewer)*

"Needed to read this! All the way through reading this book, I felt I was getting something new from it. I can suffer from excuse mode and this book has certainly helped me look at ways of overcoming this and pushing through it." - Lynda Gilroy *(Amazon.co.uk reviewer)*

"It is concise and easy to read with many helpful ideas about dealing with the potential mental pitfalls that tend to occur while running long distances. Highly recommended."- Sally Abercrombie *(Goodreads reviewer)*

Dedication

Dedicated to my mother Valli Goodale, taken too soon from this world.

Acknowledgments

I would like to thank Peter Mills and Sascha Kokott for providing important feedback on this book.

References

50 Great Myths of Popular Psychology: Shattering Widespread Misconceptions about Human Behavior by Scott O. Lilienfeld, Steven Jay Lynn, John Ruscio, and Barry L. Beyerstein, 2010

Anger Management for Dummies by W. Doyle Gentry, 2007

10 Best-Ever Depression Management Techniques by Margaret Wehrenberg, 2010

Feeling Good: The New Mood Therapy by David D. Burns, 1999

The Gift of Therapy by Irvin D. Yalom, 2002

I Don't Want to Talk About It: Overcoming the Secret Legacy of Male Depression by Terrence Real, 1997

If Men Could Talk, Here's What They'd Say by Alon Gratch, 2002

The Mindful Way through Depression: Freeing Yourself from Chronic Unhappiness by Mark Williams, John Teasdale, Zindel Segal, and John Kabat-Zinn, 2007

Psychotherapy: Lives Intersecting by Louis Breger, 2012

Quiet Your Mind & Get to Sleep by Colleen E. Carney and Rachel Manber, 2009

The Twenty-four Hour Mind: The Role of Sleep and Dreaming in Our Emotional Lives by Rosalind D. Cartwright, 2010

Undoing Depression: What Therapy Doesn't Teach You and Medication Can't Give You by Richard O'Connor, 2011